OPENING DOORS

Carole Noon and Her Dream to Save the Chimps

OPENING DOORS

Carole Noon and Her Dream to Save the Chimps

Gary Ferguson
Introduction by Jon Stryker

SAVE THE CHIMPS | Fort Pierce, Florida

Thanks to the following, who shared their time, expertise,
and/or photographs and helped make this book possible.

Allison Argo, Jeff Arnstein, Marjorie Lee Asbeck, Dr. Joceyln Bezner, Theo Capaldo,
David Cassidy, Jen Feuerstein, Gloria Grow, Martin Harvey, Linda May,
Jo-Anne McArthur, Barbara Peterson, Patti Ragan, Mika Roberts, Triana Romero,
Kay Shelton, Alec Soth, Jon Stryker, Geze Teleki, Jurek Wajdowicz

For reprint requests, media inquiries, and bulk order
discounts, please email openingdoors@savethechimps.org.

Design by LeAnna Weller Smith
Developed by Ann Treistman
Produced by Print Matters, Inc.
Printed in the United States

ISBN 978-0-979-6685-3-1

All proceeds from sales of this book will go toward the
support of Save the Chimps.

All photos courtesy of Save the Chimps,
except the following:

Jurek Wajdowicz, Emerson, Wajdowicz Studios
(EWS): 2; 82; 125; 133 top; 134

Jo-Anne McArthur: 5; 6 upper right, bottom right; 11; 12
left; 16; 25-28; 44; 45; 64; 65; 72; 74; 78; 96; 106; 108; 117;
120; 122; 135; 137; 150; 154; 158; 169; 170; 172; 175; 176

Alec Soth/Magnum Photos: 6 bottom left; 12-13 center,
15 top; 18; 19 left; 52; 59; 80; 111; 115; 118; 121; 123

Martin Harvey: 22; 39 right; 41 left; 42; 43

Courtesy of Kay Shelton and Marjorie Lee Asbeck
(Carole Noon's sisters): 30-36; 171

Barbara Peterson: 37; 38

Nicholas Tsoupis: 23 left; 39; 41 right

NASA: 50; 51; 54; 55; 56, left; 57; 58; 67

DEDICATION

With love to Dr. Carole Noon and to all the many people
she has inspired to help make this world a kinder place for
our next of kin—the amazing chimpanzee people.

CONTENTS

Foreword

FOR A NUMBER OF YEARS, ROUGHLY EVERY MONTH, I'D RECEIVE AN EMAIL FROM DR. CAROLE NOON WITH THE SUBJECT LINE "CAROLE'S CHIMP DIARY." It was Carole's way of sharing details about the chimpanzees who found freedom in our sanctuary, Save The Chimps. She had hoped one day to gather these diary entries together into a book that would tell the story of those rescued individuals.

It would be our story too of course, since our lives—Carole's, mine, and the Chimps'—became intertwined in a most unlikely and transformative way. My partnership with Carole became a deep friendship, and more often than we exchanged email, we spoke on the phone. I could almost always hear chimps in the background the way one often hears the banter of children competing for the attention of a parent distracted by a phone call from a friend. I had the sense that we were all occupying the same space. I can't speak for the Chimps, but to Carole and me, this felt like the natural order of things.

Thanks to Carole's extraordinary vision and will, none of us—not Carole, the Chimps, or I—would ever be the same again. *Opening Doors* is the story of our shared journey.

It would have made much more sense for me to meet Carole years later than I did, perhaps at a conservation conference or in some other professional context. Carole was a committed primatologist and I am the founder and president of the Arcus Foundation, a private grantmaking foundation that supports groups working globally to promote great ape conservation, and groups advancing lesbian, gay, bisexual and transgender (LGBT) human rights.

As it happened, Carole and I met through sheer happenstance. While researching great apes on the Web, my daughter and I came across a story about Dr. Noon and her efforts to gain custody of the chimpanzees who had served as test pilots for America's space program. The Air Force had plucked them from the African wilderness and used them as research subjects for medical and scientific purposes. The Air Force actually sent one of the Chimps into space to make sure the journey would be safe for humans. But as their usefulness had waned, the Air Force needed to move the Chimps along.

These chimpanzees needed an advocate, and Carole Noon was clearly up to the challenge. She had grown to know and love chimpanzees through her field work in Africa, and understood that chimps, with whom we share 97% of our DNA, feel emotions and can make and use tools. Like all of us at Arcus, she felt it was inhumane to lock them in cages. I wanted to meet with her. It was easy—in another twist of fate, she was located quite close to my home in Palm Beach, Florida.

Immediately, I saw that she had the drive and stamina to bring her dream to life. Carole opened the door for me to do one of the most important things I've done in my life. Ultimately, with support from Arcus, Save the Chimps was able to purchase land and establish itself as the largest chimpanzee sanctuary in the world. By any account, Carole succeeded in her mission, but she never had the opportunity to publish her book. She died on May 2, 2009, of pancreatic cancer. With *Opening Doors*, I hope we have done justice to her, and to the tireless work of everyone involved with protecting chimpanzees in the world.

It's important to remember that the work is not finished. While Save the Chimps provides a beautiful example of what can be done to recover lives, there are still somewhere around one thousand chimpanzees suffering behind locked doors in research facilities. Many still risk spending the vast majority of a 50-year lifespan being subjected to science rather than enjoying

society with others. For too many chimpanzees, life is about being injected, prodded, and caged rather than being held, enjoying relationships, and exploring nature. There is an urgent need for more funding to help save them, and also to keep up with the daily expenses of others in sanctuary.

I continue to believe that, if humans can find the appropriate respect for diversity among peoples and in nature, we will all survive longer as species and live better lives. I hope that the experiences described here will strengthen in you, the will and the resolve to reach that place on the horizon where our vision of a more just and humane world is fulfilled. Carole would often claim that she was just good at opening doors and that the chimpanzees did the rest. With your help, Save the Chimps will continue its job opening doors and giving sanctuary to the chimps who, thanks to Carole, have lives worth living.

JON STRYKER

Introduction

Windows to the Soul

EVERY ONE OF THEM KNOWS SOMETHING IS UP. SOMETHING BIG. THEY CAN TELL EVEN BEFORE BEING GENTLY NUDGED INTO TRAVELING CAGES, EACH HOLDING A BLANKET, AS WELL AS AN ODD ASSORTMENT OF FAVORITE THINGS: A HAT FOR TANYA, SUNGLASSES FOR EMILY, BOBBY'S FAVORITE STUFFED BEAR. A handful of people are gathered around—people they know and trust—and the humans are addressing each of them by name, over and over, saying things in gentle, encouraging voices. One of the caregivers thinks about how close she's grown to them over the past couple of years, and begins to cry.

The sun clears the east horizon to light the faces of four people rolling the cages up a small ramp, into a long trailer parked beside the metal buildings of the laboratory. Once inside, each of the ten chimps is placed next to a large window. More than anything else, it's the windows giving them a sense that this is a different sort of trip; something far removed from

their other journeys, which consisted mostly of going back and forth between biomedical labs in a closed panel truck. As the journey unfolds there will be stops every hour or so; the humans will climb into the trailer with meals or snacks of juice boxes and granola bars. Even then, most of the chimps won't be able to tear themselves away from those enthralling windows.

Chimps on the left side of the trailer can look out across Lavelle Road, to the buildings of Alamogordo some two miles away—the glass and steel of the town flashing in the sun. Beyond that the Sacramento Mountains rise in a great brown wave, not unlike the color of the peanut butter sandwiches the chimps have come to love. A few scattered clouds drift overhead. Then the two wing doors of the trailer are closed, and they hear people climbing inside the cab of the truck and shutting the doors. The engine starts. They begin to move.

At the outskirts of town, on Highway 54, the truck gains speed, rolling past great white swells of sand

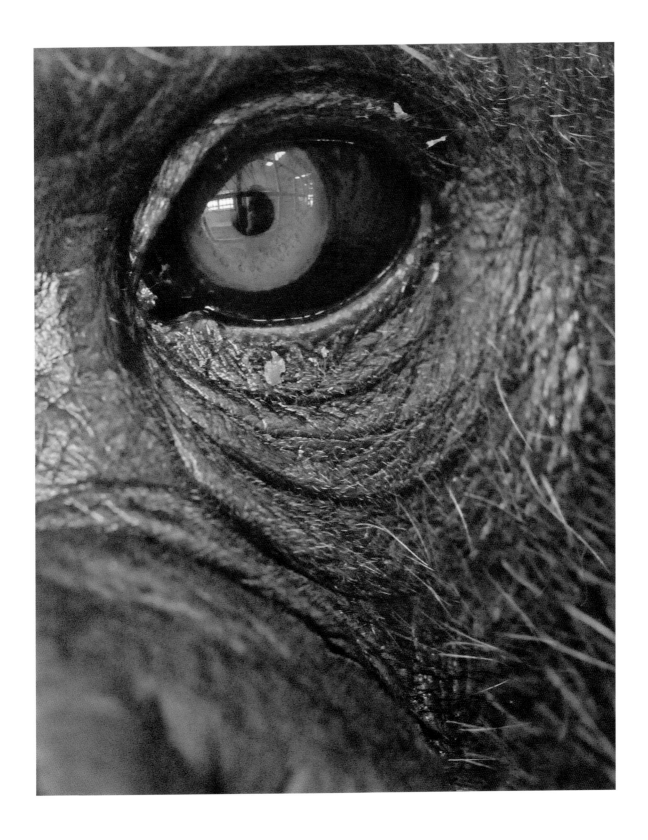

rising to the west. After an hour and a half on that lonely desert road they reach another city, a bigger one—a place called El Paso—and the rig speeds up even more, accelerating eastward onto Interstate 10. And still none of the chimps can stop looking out the windows. Even those who are tired keep rousing themselves in order not to miss anything—shaking themselves awake, propping themselves up in the cages in a way that affords good, long looks at the passing scenery.

Besides stops for treats and meals, there are other short breaks, in places where cars and trucks pull up to metal boxes and the drivers get out and pull black rubber hoses to the sides of their vehicles. During these pauses, the humans traveling with the chimps take the opportunity to come into the trailer and hand out bananas and oranges and fresh vegetables, conversing with them in the same lilting voices they used earlier that morning when the journey first began. Now and then during such stops a passerby approaches, apparently drawn to the images and words painted on the side of the trailer: Save the Chimps. Some of the onlookers carry cans of Pepsi or Barq's root beer in their hands, and the chimps acknowledge this by nodding their heads vigorously; over the past couple of years, at least

on special occasions, those same cans held treats for them too. A truck driver sees them and offers up some tangerines he has for his own meals; at a convenience store, a clerk gives them all the bananas he has on the shelf at no charge. The watchers seem delighted to find chimps looking back at them through the windows. No doubt some imagine these primate travelers to be awfully lucky, living the good life, rolling about the country in a nice trailer like a bunch of pampered tourists.

What the bystanders don't know, what they can't even imagine, is the extent to which these chimps are survivors. Refugees from what has been, for some, a

LEFT *Freddy, born in 1992 at TCF. Here he looks out the window from the trailer that brought him from the laboratory in New Mexico to the sanctuary in Florida.*

CENTER *The Coulston Foundation, once the largest captive chimpanzee colony in the world, conducted research on hundreds of animals.*

RIGHT *The custom-designed trailer used to transport the chimpanzees from New Mexico to Florida, driving more than 100,000 miles by the time everyone was moved.*

THE WINDOWS LET THEM KNOW THIS IS A DIFFERENT KIND OF TRIP.

thirty-, even forty-year sentence of fear and loneliness and despair. Surely the onlookers can't fathom wise old Rufus sitting for decades in a bare, six-by-ten-foot cage. They can't know about Amanda's troubled rocking, about Carlos's failing heart. They don't understand how significant it is for Bobby to be

reclining today in his traveling cage, showing a fair amount of calm. Born inside the Coulston Foundation (TCF) biomedical research lab at the end of January 1983, it's been an especially cruel life for Bobby. Taken from his mother when he was just twenty-two hours old, then removed from the lab nursery when he was

opening doors

OPPOSITE *Before moving to Florida, Bobby spent most of his days in a cage, alone. On his arm are signs of his self-inflicted wounds—he used his teeth to cut himself.*

LEFT TOP *The line of cages at Coulston had just enough room for a hand to reach out.*

LEFT BOTTOM *The Save the Chimps trailer drives off, its drivers working day and night to get their chimps to the sanctuary*

HE WOULD BE A SUBJECT IN EIGHT DIFFERENT RESEARCH PROJECTS— ANESTHETIZED MORE THAN 250 TIMES, HIS LIVER BIOPSIED ON AT LEAST THIRTY-FOUR OCCASIONS.

just shy of two years, he was first sent into a grinder of medical testing within the Coulston lab; later, he entered what amounted to a kind of holding facility for federally-owned surplus chimps at nearby Holloman Air Force base. During his lifetime Bobby would be a subject in eight different research projects—anesthetized more

than 250 times, his liver biopsied on at least thirty-four occasions. Like so many of the other chimps, most of his days were spent in a cage, all alone.

By 1989, Bobby was showing signs of psychosis—uncontrolled fits of screaming, and more troubling still, severely cutting his arms with his teeth, sometimes to the bone. In an attempt to help, the veterinarians wrapped his arms. They gave him diazepam, amitrip-tyline, and paroxetine. And when none of those worked, they tried Xanax, diphenhydramine, clomip-ramine, and hydroxyzine. In January 2003, Bobby became sick with thrush—a fungal disease that often starts in the mouth—while at the same time blood work indicated liver problems, including acute

"ALL WE HAVE TO DO IS GIVE THEM HALF A CHANCE,"

hepatitis. At the Coulston Foundation lab Bobby was able to take some comfort from a couple other chimps, especially a young male named Ragan; but even Ragan couldn't seem to keep him from falling back into occasional fits of self-abuse. During such times, his new caregivers would be with Bobby around the clock, trying to offer some small measure of comfort. With all that in mind, sitting today in this traveling shelter—more or less content—looking out the window, qualifies as a very good day for Bobby.

The fact that any of these chimps are smiling out their windows is in large part a testament to the newcomers—caring, intensely devoted people led by Dr. Carole Noon, who showed up at Coulston Foundation lab in 2002 to rescue them from their tortured lives. But it is a tribute as well to what appears to be a phenomenal healing ability in chimps, uniquely powerful among the world's creatures. "All we have to do is give them half a chance," Dr. Noon liked to say. "They'll do the rest."

Making things better still for the chimps heading across the country today is the fact that before leaving the lab they were given the chance to bond with one another, to be part of a family of youngsters and surrogate parents, friendly aunts and strong, silent uncles. Such coming together, which the Save the Chimps staff achieved only by providing literally hundreds of introductions across many months, will form the bedrock of their new world in Florida. Indeed, for chimpanzees, such connections hold the essence of everything implied by the word sanctuary.

THE PLACE THE CHIMPS LEFT EARLY THIS MORNING WAS A BLEAK, NONDESCRIPT COMPOUND: A CLUSTER OF LONG, NARROW SHEET METAL BUILDINGS THE COLOR OF WET SAND, SQUATTING IN THE DESERT NEXT TO THE COUNTY TRASH STATION. Yet the place was in far better shape than it once was, before Carole Noon's Save the Chimps organization came along. In those earlier years, some of the buildings featured lines of windowless doors leading to small rooms with concrete floors. Fastened to the outside of each door was a nine-by-twelve-inch Plexiglas holder into which colored pieces of paper were inserted, meant to show the level of danger from the biohazards beyond. A sheet of white paper meant that any worker could enter the room; yellow meant authorized staff only; red meant authorized staff, but only when covered

head to toe in a hazard suit. Inside the rooms were cages suspended from steel rails attached to the walls. And inside the cages were chimps, or sometimes monkeys, all in some level of experimentation, having been infected at various times with communicable diseases or injected with chemicals for toxicology studies; subjected to countless knock-downs with tranquilizer darts; and on dozens of occasions given "punch" biopsies of their livers. In the middle of the first building was a small laboratory—another plain room with bare walls. On the floor sat an operating table with restraining straps, illuminated by a swivel arm that held a blazing light cupped inside a stainless steel hood.

Elsewhere on the grounds, another building had a large open room into which lines of six-by-ten-foot cages had been constructed, one cut off from the next by solid concrete walls. The fronts of the cells were made of steel mesh onto which a feeding box had been welded to deliver doses of monkey chow. In the rear of the enclosures small doors could be opened by a human pulling on a steel cable, leading to small outdoor cages. On first arriving to the compound, Dr. Noon and her crew devoted much of their time to cleaning, scraping accumulated layers of feces from the floors and chiseling it off the walls too, where a

number of chimps, driven into various states of mental illness, had made paintings with their own waste. On first arriving here Dr. Noon found one of these buildings so dark and filthy and oppressive that she would refer to it forever more as simply "the dungeon." It was in the dungeon where Rufus spent his thirty years.

The Coulston Foundation lab had been the largest primate research facility in the nation. Like other similar facilities, the actual work done there was directed by scientists living hundreds, even thousands, of miles away. The scientists designed the experimental protocols, which were then

OPPOSITE *The long hallway in one of the Coulston buildings.*

ABOVE LEFT *Lisa, delivered at TCF by C-section, was immediately taken from her mother. Her research enrollment began at 18 months, when she was injected with ketamine at least 22 times for blood draws and throat cultures. In 2002, Lisa was saved by Save the Chimps.*

ABOVE RIGHT *Comet.*

executed by lab workers in Alamogordo. To be fair, even in the early days there'd been caring workers at Coulston. People like Millie, who ran the nursery—part of an extensive chimp breeding program at the lab—treating each little chimp as if it were her own child, pestering the vets to tend to any youngster

she found out of sorts or suffering. But young chimps were in her care only for a short time before beginning a more dire existence as test subjects elsewhere in the lab. After they left her nursery Millie often went to visit them. Sometimes she found them sad, suffering. Even now, some ten years later, that part still breaks her heart.

BY EARLY AFTERNOON THE CHIMPS ARE LOOKING OUT THEIR WINDOWS ACROSS THE BREADTH OF TEXAS, WATCHING AS MORE GREEN THINGS BEGIN TO APPEAR ON THE LAND—SEEING EVER MORE CARS AND TRUCKS ON THE ROAD, OF EVERY SIZE AND COLOR. Whenever the truck edges near a body of water, Tarzan shakes his arms and hoots an alarm;

later, when it's too dark for him to see out anymore, a caregiver named Chance comes back to play Game Boy with him. Though of course the chimps can't know it, by the wee hours they'll have started passing other biomedical research facilities—the Primate Research Center in San Antonio, and east of that the New Iberia Research Center in Lafayette, Louisiana—places that hold a portion of the roughly one thousand chimps in the United States still locked away in labs. But their route will also lead past a number of sanctuaries: the Cleveland Armory Black Beauty Ranch in Murchison, Texas, and Chimp Haven outside of Shreveport, Louisiana, as well as the Center for Great Apes in Wauchula, Florida, which offers safe haven mostly for ex-pets and former entertainment chimps and orangutans.

On it goes, for some two thousand miles, past barns and truck stops and oil derricks, past the golden arches of McDonald's, past cheatgrass and bluebonnets and barbwire fences. What each chimp actually notices, the things he or she chooses to focus on, is—much as it would be for us—driven to a great degree by personality. Tanya may be spending a lot of her time just looking up, satisfied by the broad and cloudless sky; for some reason, Tanya's always at her best in full sun, with no hint of approaching storms. Jaybee, on the other hand, is a climber. It's easy to imagine the appearance of white oak and elm and beech near the Louisiana border sparking in him an extraordinary sense of delight.

For some long-time residents of the laboratory, though, all this fresh scenery fails to spark any urge to be out there exploring. No matter the terrible conditions they suffered, for decades cages of one sort or another have been home for them; and home, no matter how foul, isn't something everyone can throw off so easily. Dr. Noon and her staff realized this after watching an earlier group from Coulston arrive at Save the Chimps in Florida. At the sanctuary each chimpanzee house is joined to its own sun-drenched island by a grassy walkway. Early on, though, some of the chimps were afraid to leave the familiar concrete and steel mesh of the buildings. So the decision was made to install a strip of chain-link fence panels leading from the house to the islands. That's all it took. Even the most reluctant among them made their way, keeping one hand on the chain link as they moved along, each step just a little more confident than the last.

INSPIRED BY THE WORK OF
JANE GOODALL, CAROLE FOUND
HER WAY TO A CHIMP SANCTUARY
IN ZAMBIA

YEARS BEFORE THESE CHIMPANZEE ROAD TRIPS GOT UNDER WAY, CAROLE NOON, HAVING BEEN INSPIRED BY THE WORK OF JANE GOODALL, FOUND HER WAY TO A SPLENDID CHIMP SANCTUARY IN ZAMBIA KNOWN AS THE CHIMFUNSHI WILDLIFE ORPHANAGE, RUN BY DAVID AND SHEILA SIDDLE. Designed to accommodate chimps seized in the illegal pet and bushmeat trades, Chimfunshi would become a splendid obsession for Dr. Noon; across roughly a decade she would spend nearly four years there, including a nine month stretch devoted to completing her PhD. At one point Jane Goodall asked Carole to go to Chimfunshi to check in on a chimp named Milla, whom she had rescued and placed at the sanctuary.

"When Milla came to Chimfunshi," Carole later recalled, "she was an 18-year-old female. The traditional thinking back then was, 'She's doomed—there's no way to introduce an 18-year-old female into a social group.' I knew better, and I know better now because we're introducing 45-year-old females. Just because they sit in a box for 40 years doesn't mean they're empty inside. When you open the door and they walk through it, they meet every challenge. They know what they're doing. They're ready to get on with their lives."

In 1997, shortly after returning to Florida from Africa, Carole got her first real chance to resocialize chimps in the United States. And that chance came in astonishing fashion. Having heard of government plans to send 141 of the pioneer chimps of the U.S. space program to a biomedical lab, she sued the Air Force. Following a thorny, protracted legal battle, she was given custody of twenty-one of those primate heroes. Many were in bad shape: Dana and Faith had lost their hair; Hannah couldn't stop rocking. Getting those twenty-one chimps out of the lab and giving them sanctuary in Florida was a magnificent accomplishment, one that could have provided Carole with plenty of work for years to come. But soon after those first chimps arrived there would come another, even bigger miracle—a seed that would grow into what's become the largest chimpanzee rescue sanctuary in the world. In the end there would be twenty-seven of these trips from the lab in Alamogordo to the sanctuary in Fort Pierce, the round trip journeys adding up to more than a hundred thousand miles. Or, as Carole sometimes thought of it, like driving four times around the planet, and then some.

OF THE NEARLY FIVE THOUSAND SPECIES OF MAMMALS ON EARTH, THE CHIMPANZEE IS THE ONE MOST LIKE US, SHARING A PHENOMENAL 98 PERCENT OF OUR GENES. Indeed, many anthropologists and geneticists believe that millions of years ago humans and chimps split from a common ancestor. That's maybe why it is nearly impossible to be around chimpanzees even for a few minutes without sensing a whole host of things that seem uncannily familiar. We've now known for decades that chimpanzees experience much of what we do, including fear and laughter, depression and

HOW IS IT THAT WE COULD SO PROFOUNDLY MISTREAT THEM?

insecurity, eagerness and anger. They can anticipate. They can master a wide variety of tools—from a socket wrench to a computer keyboard—in relatively little time. They can learn sign language, using it for everything from complaining about food they don't like, to commenting about the fact that a caregiver has lost weight.

OPPOSITE *Clean blankets drying on the line at Save the Chimps. Blankets are important for the chimpanzees, who use them to make comfortable sleeping nests.*

LEFT *Jersey grooming Dalton.*

With all that, of course, comes an inescapable question: If chimps are so like us, if they serve as an obvious bridge between us and the life we share this planet with, and if in so many cases they've been pressed into service either for our entertainment or to advance our quest for knowledge, how is it that we could so profoundly mistreat them? Of course humans have routinely mistreated one another as well. Homeless people were once used for lobotomy experiments; more recently, indigent black men in Alabama were injected with syphilis without their

knowledge so researchers could learn more about the course of the disease. But thankfully, as such callous, misguided efforts in the name of science were brought to light, we became outraged at the inhumanity of it. It remains to be seen whether or not we can extend that compassion to a beautiful primate who also happens to be our closest relative.

In the later years of his life, the great mythologist Joseph Campbell talked often about the problem of a culture like ours that had turned its back on its guiding stories and myths. He meant the big stories, the kind that for thousands of years served as the sparks needed to light our better natures. During conversations with journalists, Campbell was often asked if he foresaw a day when a new body of myth and story might emerge. Yes, he replied. It will arise out of a view of Earth much as the astronauts saw it: the planet as a fragile ball of life hurtling through the dark void, bereft of all boundary lines and political fences. Earth, in other words, at last understood as a fabulous web of connections, a place where what we do to one thread in the fabric, has consequences for all the rest.

This, then, is that kind of story.

OPENING DOORS

Carole Noon and Her Dream to Save the Chimps

GLENVIEW
BAY VILLAGE OHIO
GRADE 3
MRS LINABURY

FEBRUARY 19 1958
OHIO SCHOOL PICTURES
BEREA, OHIO

CHAPTER 01

The Woman Behind the Chimps

I F FOR SOME STRANGE REASON YOU HAPPENED TO STUMBLE ACROSS A CERTAIN 1958 BLACK-AND-WHITE PHOTO OF MRS. LINABURY'S THIRD GRADE CLASS AT GLENVIEW ELEMENTARY SCHOOL IN BAY VILLAGE, OHIO, YOU MIGHT BE TEMPTED TO LINGER OVER IT—if only to ponder the eager look of small town America in the 1950s. Standing in front of a line of blackboards are thirty-one scrubbed young faces, along with a properly bookish-looking, middle-aged teacher. It being class photo day, the children have been carefully wrapped in plaid skirts and sailor blouses and bright white bobby socks, in sports coats and bow ties and sweater vests.

Look a little longer, and your attention may come to rest on one child in particular—a small blonde girl at the end of the top row standing next to Mrs. Linabury, wearing a beige sweater and a pageboy haircut that extends to her collar. What makes her compelling is her expression: head tilted to the side a few degrees and one of her dark eyebrows raised slightly in a pensive look that seems to belie a mix of supreme confidence and quiet amusement. As if at nine years old, Carole Noon already knows something we don't; or, at the very least, is driven by something not everyone has the good fortune to encounter.

ABOVE *Carole's friends took this posed photograph of her before her first trip to Africa. She's holding a brochure from the tour group, "Adventures International." Sitting on the steps are the* Whole Earth Catalog *and* Snake Bite Treatments; *her dog, Zeke, sits behind her.*

OPPOSITE *Carole Noon's third-grade class photo. She is the first child in the top row.*

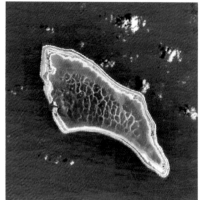

ABOVE LEFT *The 140-foot yacht that housed Carole's father's offices, anchored at Kanton Island. He and his partner were in Kanton to salvage the* President Taylor, *a ship that had run aground while entering the lagoon. The intent was to sell the scrap metal.*

ABOVE RIGHT *Kanton Island.*

In truth, she does know a few things that most of the rest of 1950s Ohio doesn't. Five years earlier her father and several of his business partners decided to relocate their offices to a 140-foot yacht anchored at the edge of a tiny tropical island in the South Pacific, halfway between Hawaii and Fiji. Kanton Island is a coral atoll, thirty miles around, nine miles long, and very narrow in parts. Shaped something like a pork chop, and surrounding a pristine lagoon, the island at the time had about a hundred residents. In addition to a store and a hotel, there was an airport refueling station. The airline personnel were among the island's few residents, there to service the planes flying from Honolulu to Australia. (Planes in those days were not yet able to carry enough fuel to make a non-stop flight.) There was a doctor and dentist who came to the island twice a year.

For some fifteen months, Carole and her two older sisters ran free under the coconut palms (planted by the residents), past the fan flowers, on the hot coral where scant vegetation grew, and up and down the graceful sandy beaches, following turtles and lizards and hermit crabs, casting lines into the lagoon in hopes of catching one of the more than 150 species of fish living there. Carole was impish and carefree. So thoroughly native did the girls become during the course

the woman behind the chimps

TOP LEFT,
BOTTOM LEFT,
CENTER
*Carole and friends
on Kanton Island.*

FAR RIGHT
In college.

of their stay that in the end their mother decided a little civilization might be in order, moving them first to Honolulu, and later to the Midwest.

According to her sister Lee, Carole's dramatic response to Disney's animated film, "Lady and the Tramp," was telling: "When Tramp was whisked off to the pound, Carole wept almost uncontrollably. That he was later freed through the efforts of a purebred cocker spaniel and given a home, did little to abate her outrage." As a middle schooler, Carole valiantly fought to save a poisoned backyard mole. Unfortunately, he expired in a dresser drawer that he shared with socks and tee shirts.

She was always following her fancies. Following her gut. Oblivious to notions of what girls could and couldn't do.

That ability to rise above what people said could or should be done, combined with an astonishing degree of focus, were at the core of Carole's personality. But she also had in the mix a rascally playfulness, including a razor-sharp sense of humor—dry as toast and generally unfriendly to fools. Such traits flowered in high school, where she was known to many as "the class wit." In hindsight, looking at the fiercely driven nature of her life and the scrutiny she brought to nearly every waking

hour, it might be safe to say that this wit was what kept her standing. It may even have been what kept her sane.

When Carole Noon got angry—and without question, even back then she sometimes wore a short fuse—it was often her cats and dogs who did the soothing. There was a toy poodle named Holden, named after the main character in *The Catcher in the Rye*; a cat named Alice, named after *Alice's Restaurant*; and another big black cat called Korczak, for the sculptor in South Dakota who had taken up the task of chiseling a likeness of Crazy Horse out of the side of a mountain.

Carole would eventually move from Ohio to Boynton Beach, Florida, where her sister was living, leaving behind both the carpet cleaning business she'd begun with her then-husband Michael, as well as the marriage, which had ended in divorce. Enrolling in classes at a local community college she dove into zoology, biology, and physics before

SHE WAS ALWAYS FOLLOWING HER FANCIES. FOLLOWING HER GUT.

ABOVE AND RIGHT
Carole in her youth.

transferring first to Florida Atlantic University, and later to the University of Florida. "Her thought was to get a degree to become a wildlife biologist, or something along those lines," says her sister Lee. While at Florida Atlantic, though, she happened to meet another animal-loving student like herself—a graduate student in anthropology named Barbara Peterson. "We clicked immediately," Barbara says. "The chemistry between us was great. I loved her attitude. Her sense of humor was obvious from the beginning." When Barbara told Carole that Jane Goodall was coming to campus—an event sponsored by the anthropology department—and then invited her to attend a cocktail party with Goodall after the lecture, Carole didn't wait to be asked twice.

By the time of this particular lecture, in 1981, Goodall had long been both a compelling scientist and storyteller, infusing rigorous scientific work with a passionate, unwavering commitment to

advocacy. What's more, she'd started from modest beginnings, working as a secretary in Africa when she happened to meet celebrated paleontologist Louis Leakey. Impressed by her enthusiasm and intelligence, Leakey ended up sending Goodall to London to study primate behavior and anatomy with pioneer researchers Osmon Hill and John Napier. Jane would return to Africa, to Gombe Stream National Park, shortly after a U.S. expedition had finished slashing through the dark forests of Cameroon, capturing more than five dozen infant chimpanzees for the American space program.

"Carole and I met Jane at that cocktail party," Barbara says. "For some reason Jane asked if we'd be interested in helping out with the ChimpanZoo project she was starting." The aim of ChimpanZoo—a program eventually launched in zoos and animal parks across the country—was to use volunteers to document the behavior of chimps in various settings, from wild populations to traditional zoos. Lion Country had what was called a "semi-feral" population of chimps—a description based on the fact that while people were allowed to drive through the park and observe from their cars, the chimps weren't bound by traditional cages and, as a result, had a minimal amount of close interaction with humans.

The day after Goodall's lecture, Carole and Barbara drove with her to Lion Country to get a better sense of the project. With encouragement from two sisters (along with their generous standing offer to take care of her dogs and cats), Carole joined the effort. That was the first of many such drives Barbara and Carole would make in the months that followed, sharing long talks on the road, beginning what would become a lifelong friendship. At one point the two women had the bright idea of making money by collecting elephant poop and then selling it to gardeners at garage sales. "I think we called it 'zoo poop,' or something like that," Barbara recalls. "At any rate, the poop ended up on two gardens—mine and hers."

The ChimpanZoo project required long periods of observation, the volunteers using clipboards fitted with gridded paper to record the time and location of various chimp behaviors. "I saw identical looking dark blurs," Carole recalls of her first time observing the chimps, "doing pretty much nothing at all." But she poured herself into the work, and before long the chimps' personalities became obvious to her. The rules by which the chimps lived, as she described it later, began to reveal themselves:

"Two chimps have a fight. Then it starts to rain. Well, if there's only one shelter available and you want to get out of the storm, this calls for some fancy politics. Those chimpanzees had worked it all out."

One day on leaving the park she glanced back to see the chimps in her rear view mirror. "A few of them had gotten up and moved to the edge of their little world to watch me leave. I was going home to do whatever I wanted, go wherever I wanted. And they were staying right where they were."

Following Goodall's lecture at Florida Atlantic University, Carole had a chance to talk with the primatologist about what it would take to pursue such work as a profession. Jane's advice, drawn from her own experience, was kind but blunt: "If you want to work for the benefit of animals," she

ABOVE *Jane Goodall, left, with Carole at ChimpanZoo, observing chimpanzees.*

said, "you need to either be a lawyer or get your PhD. That's what you'll need in order for people to take you seriously."

That was good enough for Carole. She started steering in that direction, working through first her master's degree, then gaining actual experience with chimpanzees through her doctoral work at the Chimfunshi Wildlife Orphanage in Africa. The more she learned, the more entrenched that image in her rear view mirror of the chimps in Florida, at Lion Country Safari, became. How does a creature with such an elaborate social life, she wondered, with a physical body meant for vigorous traveling, with a brain able to hold complex maps of wide-ranging territory, manage to survive in captivity?

That question, in turn, led her to others, including why we keep chimpanzees in captivity in the first place. Those in zoos, she knew, were held up as ambassadors of their species, purportedly to inspire such a sense of awe in the public that they end up wanting to save chimps in the wild. Still others served as stand-ins in the laboratory, used for experiments we'd never consider performing on one another—research that supposedly benefited us with medical breakthroughs but which over the decades had yielded surprisingly little. The final reason for keeping

chimps was to sell products on TV or to amuse us in the movies—at least until the hairy little child actors grew up and become hard to handle. "Captive chimpanzees work for a living," Carole wrote. "They all have jobs. They serve us. Until a few are lucky enough to be retired to a bona fide sanctuary where humans serve them."

"After Chimfunshi," says Barbara Peterson, "Carole knew she wanted to work in a sanctuary." Yet for all her determination, there were days when she admitted being discouraged, wondering how she'd ever pull off such a lofty goal. "I told her to be patient," Barbara said. "I told her one day it would happen."

"AFTER CHIMFUNSHI, CAROLE KNEW SHE WANTED TO WORK IN A SANCTUARY."

CAROLE'S FORMER HUSBAND MICHAEL ONCE GAVE HIS WIFE A NICKNAME. IT WAS "NOT AFRAID OF THE WOODS." A PERFECT FIT, REALLY. Because while the woods—or poachers or chimp breeders or bad biomedical labs—may have overwhelmed Carole at times, even left her now and then quietly second-guessing herself, one thing they never seemed to do, at least not for long, was to keep her afraid. No doubt what many people will remember about Carole is her intensity; her stubbornness. But she was also con-stantly asking other people for their opinions about chimps and chimpanzee care (though if your opinion was different from hers, it had better come wrapped in ironclad reasoning). Through such conversations she was on the lookout for any stones she might have left unturned, trying to find out if there was new information out there that might influence her final decisions. But the final decisions were always hers.

"When you're that focused," says friend and colleague Dr. Theo Capaldo of Carole, "when you

"HE WAS AWKWARD, HE WAS HOLDING ON FOR DEAR LIFE, HIS KNUCKLES WERE WHITE, HE WAS SCARED OUT OF HIS MIND…BUT HE WAS SO DARNED CURIOUS."

climbing and swinging and grooming and lounging up in the leaf canopy, Toby was stuck down on the ground, looking up. So it went, day after day. Still, Carole had no doubt that one day Toby would overcome his dread. "Any day now," she wrote in her notes, "Toby's going to climb." Yet, because she was

about to leave Chimfunshi for the States, she concluded sadly that Toby's big day would probably be without her around to celebrate with him.

Then, as she described it, "Damned if he didn't get up and climb the tree. And he climbed it exactly the way I imagined I would climb it: he was awkward, he was holding on for dear life, his knuckles were white, he was scared out of his mind. But he was so darned curious about what was going on up there, what everybody was doing, that he did it."

It was a perfect example of the kind of curiosity that years later she would see expressed over and over again, as she watched both former residents of the Coulston Foundation lab—some having been locked away and isolated in concrete cells for thirty or more years—as well as several former pets who had come to Save the Chimps, find their way out onto the open, grassy islands she helped build for them. When it was time to release former pets April and September to their island, for example, they were extremely hesitant, but in the end were able to use one another to build confidence. For a long time both sat in the doorway, unsure of what to do; finally, April found the courage to at least walk over and check out the adjacent patio. And from there she managed to tiptoe a few feet onto that strange-looking green stuff called grass. September, watching her friend from the doorway, and seeing that nothing bad had happened to her, headed out to the grass to investigate. In no time she was digging, discovering much to her amazement that there was something under that grass called dirt. She just kept digging, gently holding each handful of soil up to her nose and sniffing it, then carefully putting it in a pile next to the growing hole. "Of course," said Carole, "September's holes will fill with rainwater and make mud all over the place. I don't even care about the mess. September came out of the cage."

Carole devoted a lot of energy to exploring whether or not it was possible to predict how chimps would act toward one another when finally given the opportunity to socialize. Since battles between hostile chimps can result in serious injuries, even death, the question had great significance for those running primate sanctuaries. Notably, at the end of her dissertation work at Chimfunshi, she concluded that in fact there was no foolproof formula. "Chimpanzees are people," she would say. And for them, much like for us, "sometimes the chemistry between two individuals is good, sometimes it's bad. Sometimes it goes from one to the other."

Despite not finding any formula, Carole proved incredibly skillful at "simply opening doors," as she often described her work. And that was due, in large part, to her astonishing ability to pay attention to the smallest details of chimp behavior, achieved by spending thousands of hours with them day and night. Her decisions—which to others may have seemed to arise from gut feelings—were in fact the fruit of a kind of fierce mindfulness.

In January 2005—well after Save the Chimps Sanctuary had become a splendid reality—Carole wrote a happy New Year letter to Sheila and David Siddle, whom she referred to affectionately as "Ma and Pa." She was commenting on something Sheila said in a previous note, sent to congratulate Carole on winning the Jane Goodall Award for Lifetime Dedication to the Care of Chimpanzees, suggesting that she needed no help from anyone to reach the success she currently enjoyed. "This is pretty funny," Carole wrote back, "coming from the person who taught me so much of what I know." If Jane Goodall had pointed her in the right direction, she said, then Sheila and David deserved credit "for showing me all the gory details of that direction.

"I pretty much hold you and Pa responsible for this mess I have gotten myself into. I arrived at Chimfunshi book smart (remember, I'm the one who knew what the initials DNA stood for) AND with chimpanzee experience—a winning combination. You and Spencer and Charlie and Sandy, and of course Rita and dear Jimmy, and Dora and Pan and Goblin and dear Grumps and Mike and Miss Pick Pocket Pippa, now adults, and all the others, taught me the rest."

LEFT AND BELOW *Chimpanzees at Chimfunshi.*

have that much intentionality and intelligence in your focus, it equals a kind of certainty. It really doesn't matter whether or not other people disagree." And for the particular job Carole would end up taking on, that sort of intensity would prove to be an awfully handy thing.

For all her focus, though, those close to Carole Noon also describe her as droll and smart and sincere and vulnerable. Upon being diagnosed with cancer, one of Carole's little pleasures while bedridden was watching Judge Judy on TV. "I don't like confrontation," she told her friend Patti Ragan, director of the Center for Great Apes. "I try to make everybody feel better even when I'm firing them. I need to watch Judge Judy every day 'cause I have to toughen up."

Something of these qualities, too, would play out in the mix of what came to occupy her mind nearly every waking hour, which was how to better tend to the welfare of chimpanzees—or "people," as she always called them. You can find it in the way she shared with other sanctuaries her discoveries

opening doors

about everything from designs for better chimp enclosures to food recipes; or in notes she wrote to her staff, thanking them for throwing the chimps a terrific holiday party; or in the messages she exchanged with her dear friend and key supporter, Arcus Foundation founder Jon Stryker—times when it seemed to dawn on her that the world really was moving a little to accommodate their outrageous intentions. You could have also seen it time and again late at night, when she could be found sitting in the shelter building with one hand around a Budweiser or Miller Lite, the fingers of the other hand touching the fingers of Dana the chimp, the two of them working out thorny problems into the wee hours.

the woman behind the chimps

PHYLLIS

"SHE WAS ONE OF THE ORIGINAL AIR FORCE CHIMPS THAT ARRIVED IN 2001, AND WE SORT OF GREW OLD TOGETHER," SAID CAROLE.

IT'S BEEN YEARS SINCE PHYLLIS SAW PEOPLE OPENING THE BACK DOORS OF THAT TRAILER AFTER THE LONG JOURNEY EAST FROM NEW MEXICO—SAW THEM STANDING THERE WITH GREAT BIG SMILES ON THEIR FACES, SAYING, "WELCOME TO FLORIDA!" It was the beginning of a life so different from what she'd known that she might as well have gotten out of a spaceship onto another planet. Her mother was Anna, captured in Africa as a baby and pressed into service for the American space program—one day to be strapped into metal chairs and accelerated and spun and heated and all manner of other things intended to figure out what bodies could endure. Anna gave birth to Phyllis in the laboratory and was allowed to be with her just ten minutes before her daughter was placed in a nursery where for a time, along with other chimpanzees, she was raised by humans.

The first time Phyllis was anesthetized she was a year old, put down so that the number "630" could be tattooed on her chest. Over the course of the next thirty-two years she was given anesthetics another 234 times—mostly for drawing blood and for performing biopsies and ultrasounds. She was barely two when she entered her first research study, which involved what's often referred to as "chair training." This required strapping her legs and head into a large metal restraining chair, in front of which were two levers—one to her left, the other on her right. Lights were flashed in front of her, at which point she was supposed to choose the correct lever to pull—the one on the right if the light was green, and the one on the left if the light was red. If she made the right choice she got a sip of water, maybe a banana pellet; if she chose the wrong one, she was given an electrical shock to the soles of her feet.

This eventually led to a similar study, this one involving "couch training." For that she was placed in a suit covering her torso, which was then tightly laced to a horizontal metal frame in order to keep her from escaping. She spent her third birthday pinned to the couch for just under sixteen hours. The experience was so unpleasant that she squirmed constantly, ultimately tearing deep lesions in her legs from rubbing them against the edges of the torso suit. The

injuries proved so serious that, in the end, she was pulled from the study.

Next came a year of hepatitis study, which included being knocked out dozens of times in order to perform biopsies on her liver. That, in turn, was followed by clinical tests for a gonorrhea study, which meant putting her out many more times in order to take samples of her blood.

Then, in 1976, when Phyllis was nine years old she was shuffled into what was known as the National Chimpanzee Breeding Program. Her sole job was to produce more research subjects for the lab. She was paired with a male for a few weeks, and if she didn't become pregnant she was put in with another male chimp instead. Phyllis lived alone until the babies came; half of the ten youngsters she birthed were

stillborn. Even though lab reports indicate she was a good parent, Phyllis's babies were taken away from her within hours, or at most within days, of their birth, much as had happened with her own mother. The medical records note how depressed Phyllis was after these separations; strangely, the comments about this in the reports seem bemused, showing not a hint of anyone knowing what might have caused the problem.

She was thirty-two years old when the testing and the mating and the biopsies and the blood drawing and the electric shocks finally came to an end, thanks to the arrival of Dr. Noon and her staff. And in time, like all the chimps at Coulston, Phyllis would be driven across the country to Florida, where she found many of the chimps she'd known

out West: Marty, Emory, Gromek, and Wes were there—all of whom she'd been paired with for weeks at a time for breeding. Emily and Jennifer were there, too, both of whom spent lots of effort trying to cheer her up during her deep depressions after her babies were taken away.

"She was one of the original Air Force chimps that arrived in 2001, and we sort of grew old together," said Carole. Talking about Phyllis near the end of the chimp's life, Carole reflected on how she and the rest of the staff were in many ways running a hospice. "Almost a hundred of the chimpanzees are over 30 years old, and they've all been compromised by their biomedical past." The reason that fact hadn't left the staff in a constant state of sadness was because for every death there were wonderful flushes of life to behold. Jaybee was now running on an island with his new best friend, Kiley. Juan, Mack, Carlos, and Casey, all of whom had been living alone in Building 300—the dungeon—were now living on big islands with big families. Phyllis's daughter Jersey was in Florida, too, and the caregivers would likely have another forty years to pamper and spoil her.

"The tragedy isn't that Carrie, Phyllis, and others are gone after years of doing our best for them," Carole said after Phyllis died. "The tragedy would have been if they had been left behind at Coulston to face a life of more of the same."

Space Heroes

I N 1962, AMERICA WAS CELEBRATING ITS SUCCESSES IN SPACE
EXPLORATION. AT THE BEGINNING OF THE YEAR, JOHN GLENN, JR.
BECAME THE FIRST AMERICAN TO ORBIT EARTH, which he did
three times in the space of about five hours. Glenn, however, was not
the first primate to orbit the earth. He was preceded by Enos, the
second chimpanzee sent into space.

Yet it was Glenn, along with his fellow astronauts Alan Shepard
and Gus Grissom, who were celebrated by four million New Yorkers
in a stunning parade on Broadway, their convertible showered with
more than twelve tons of ticker tape. Carole Noon, thirteen years old
at the time, recalled reading about the event in the newspaper and
feeling a flush of pride: "They were our heroes back then. They were
real American heroes." And when Carole later learned the fate of the
chimpanzees, most of whom ended up as subjects for various chemical
and biomedical experiments, she would be outraged for the rest of
her life: "While the astronauts were getting their ticker tape parade,
the Air Force was reassigning the chimpanzees to hazardous research
environment. I was still convinced that if their story got out to most of
America, most of America would be as appalled as I was."

There are scant records about how the military actually went
about securing wild chimps for the space program. But as Carole

ABOVE *Al Worden, Apollo 15 astronaut,
tours Save the Chimps. Here he speaks to
director Jen Feuerstein.*

OPPOSITE *The Friendship 7 mission
takes off, carrying John Glenn, Jr., on
his historic orbit of the earth.*

ABOVE *The facilities at the Holloman Air Force Base in Alamogordo, where the chimpanzees for the space program were kept while they were being used by NASA.*

OPPOSITE *Thoto in the grass at Save the Chimps in Fort Pierce. His blanket is behind him, and he's playing with a doll—two comforts that were never provided for the chimps at Holloman or the Coulston Foundation.*

later discovered, the prevailing method employed by bush trappers—a method still used today—was an especially vicious one, involving the gunning down of mothers literally right out from under their infants, then also shooting any adults who became aggressive. "Most of the [space] chimps Carole was later awarded from the military were illegally obtained from the Congo," explains Geza Teleki, who for decades worked to expose the illegal trade of great apes in Western Africa. "The Air Force made a deal with Congo President Mobutu under the table. Then all they had to do was send over transport planes. Those particular chimps never even went through customs."

It was harsh treatment, especially for chimps who for a time were routinely touted by the press as heroes. And it got no better in the years that followed. Some died during training. And of those who survived, all but a very few would find themselves shoved into biomedical labs, living alone in concrete and steel cages. There they would languish for more than thirty years—never putting their feet in the grass, never sleeping under the stars, never even being allowed to spend time with their own babies. Not until, that is, Carole Noon came along.

Mission:
TO SURVIVE

I'T'S NEARLY DAYBREAK ON THE LAST DAY OF JANUARY 1961. AT CAPE CANAVERAL, FLORIDA, A MERCURY REDSTONE ROCKET SITS ON A LAUNCH PAD, THE EXHAUST GASES FROM THE ENGINES CHURNING INTO THE COOL MORNING AIR. Strapped into a capsule at the top of the rocket is a five-year-old, thirty-seven-pound astronaut, firmly secured into a pod-shaped, four-foot-tall plastic casing. Though his original name was Chang, the world would come to know him as Ham, or just as often as "Ham the Astrochimp." The moniker came not from any sort of personality trait, as in someone who enjoys showing off might be called a "ham," but rather as shorthand for Holloman Aerospace Medical Center. His mission is to ascend 115 miles into suborbital space, then travel downrange a distance of 290 miles before splashing down in the Atlantic Ocean, all the while performing tasks meant to verify that his mental functions—especially his reaction time—are still intact. Mostly, though, his mission is to survive. If he does, it will be a major step forward in the nation's quest to put a human in orbit around the Earth.

Arriving in the United States in 1959, at the age of three, Ham trained at Holloman Air Force Base in Alamogordo, New Mexico, along with sixty-four other chimps. Each started life in the wilds of West Africa, clinging to their mothers as all little ones do, roaming the rich forests with their clans of thirty or forty chimps, following the seasons of ripening fruit, digging for termites, defending the borders of their territories, playing and grooming and sleeping in the tree canopies. But all that came to a fast end when the

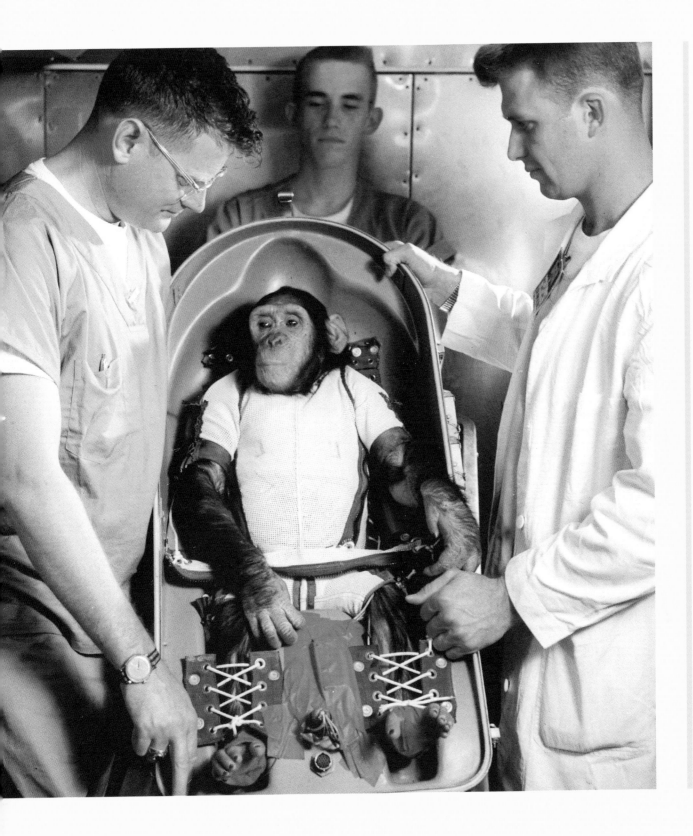

THE PHYSICAL AND MENTAL TRAINING HAM AND HIS FELLOW CHIMPS UNDERGO AT HOLLOMAN IS NOTHING SHORT OF EXTRAORDINARY

United States launched an expedition to capture infant chimpanzees for the space program.

The physical and mental training Ham and his fellow chimps undergo at Holloman is nothing short of extraordinary: placed in centrifuges to see how many g-forces they can endure; given regular rides on rocket sleds, which sometimes decelerate so quickly that chimps die from heart failure or brain hemorrhages; they're locked in decompression chambers until they lose consciousness; and finally, they spend countless hours strapped into "the couch," as the confinement shells where they were trained and later secured in the rocket capsule were called, made to push a certain lever within five seconds of seeing a corresponding flashing light. When they get it right, they earn a banana pellet; when they get it wrong, they get an electric shock to the souls of their feet.

On the day of Ham's launch, there are problems. They begin shortly after dawn, when a computer glitch keeps the rocket sitting on the pad for six hours, not blasting off until almost noon. Furthermore, while the ship was predicted to achieve a top speed of 4,200 mph, exposing Ham to a maximum of 11 g of acceleration force, in fact he

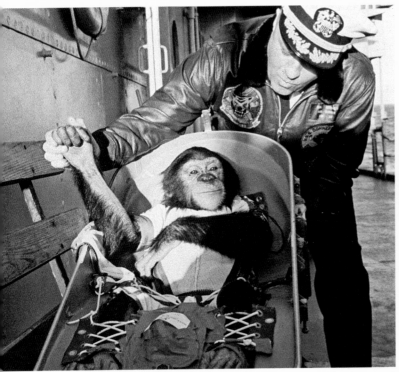

ABOVE AND LEFT
More photographs of Ham.

will end up enduring more than fourteen—the equivalent of his body suddenly growing in weight to more than five hundred pounds. Shortly after breaking into the upper atmosphere, the capsule suffers partial pressure loss—a situation Ham manages to survive thanks to the fact that he's wearing a pressurized suit.

Sixteen minutes after launch Ham splashes down into the Atlantic. It's a rough landing, though, very rough, and soon after touchdown the capsule begins taking on water; thankfully, the support crew manages to reach Ham in time. When they open the hatch there he is, nose bruised from the impact of the splashdown, but otherwise apparently okay, wearing what to those watching at home on their black-and-white televisions looks like an enormous smile. His expression brings relief to many, including journalists, who say that it shows he really

enjoyed his wild ride—that even for a chimpanzee, it was the adventure of a lifetime. What they don't know is that in the world of chimps this particular look, lips curled back to reveal the teeth, isn't a smile at all, but an expression of extraordinary fear. Jane Goodall would later say that she'd never seen a chimpanzee so abjectly terrified.

As the flashbulbs fire all around him, Ham seems to take it all in stride. One photo setup the handlers try to arrange, however, that involves placing him back in "the couch" he strongly resists. An image from that day appears on the February 10, 1961 cover of LIFE magazine, with the headline "Back from Space: A Confident 'Ham.'" NASA, too, seems justifiably proud of their little flyer, pointing out that "Ham's survival, despite a host of harrowing mischances . . . [has] raised the confidence of the astronauts and the capsule engineers alike."

BELOW AND RIGHT *Enos took Ham's place in the 1961 test flight to orbit the Earth. Here are two postcards that feature the chimpanzee, and a picture of him with one of his NASA handlers.*

ENOS *the Astronaut Chimpanzee*   ENOS *the Astronaut Chimpanzee*

AFTER HAM'S SUCCESSFUL TRIP INTO SUB-ORBITAL SPACE, MORE FLIGHTS WITH PRIMATES SOON FOLLOWED. In November of 1961, a one-and-a-half-pound squirrel monkey named Goliath was launched into the sky atop an Atlas rocket; tragically, thirty-five seconds later there was a malfunction and the rocket was intentionally destroyed. (It's worth mentioning that by this time monkeys in general had suffered big losses in their role as flight pioneers. These began with the suffocation death of Albert I, a rhesus monkey sent up in a V2 rocket in the summer of 1948. Three days later, Albert II went up, surviving the flight only to die on impact during

landing. Albert III made for the skies in December of 1949, but on reaching an altitude of 35,000 feet the rocket exploded. Still another rhesus monkey, Albert IV, had a successful flight in the spring of 1950, but he, too, was killed during landing.)

Despite the disaster with Goliath, by the end of 1961 NASA was closing in on the major goal of the Mercury missions—to actually orbit the Earth. Before placing a human in the capsule, though, there would be one more chimp flight, and once again Ham was picked for the mission. Oddly, though, shortly before the day of the launch he managed to get into a bag of banana pellets

LEFT *A chimpanzee peers through the bars of its window in one of the Coulston Foundation's facilities.*

and eat himself silly, ending up overweight and forcing NASA to find a replacement. Among the handful of other chimpanzees fully trained for the Mercury missions, the scientists chose a five-year-old named Enos, also born in Africa. Like Ham, Enos had no shortage of the right stuff. Shortly after launch on November 28, 1961, a malfunction in the capsule caused him to receive an electric shock not when he made a wrong choice at the controls—a foundation of space chimp training—but rather when he made the right choice. Incredibly, Enos endured this, continuing to make the right choices throughout the flight, landing after two orbits around the Earth. And with that accomplishment the path was finally clear for John Glenn, who in 1962 became the first American to orbit the planet.

Being a celebrity of sorts, after his mission, Ham would at least get to spend some of his time at the National Zoo. And while he unfortunately lived there alone—never a good situation for a chimpanzee—in the final years of his life he was transferred to a zoo in Charlotte, North Carolina, where at long last he became part of a family group—one of the few times he'd known such comfort since being taken from his family in Africa decades before. Yet if Ham

RIGHT *Marlon with blanket.*

gained a measure of retirement, that was hardly the case for many of the other, less celebrated space chimps. Enos died several months after his flight after contracting dysentery. Minnie—who was Ham's backup and the only female chimp trained for space flight in the Mercury program—would stay in biomedical labs for more than thirty years, spending much of that time as part of a breeding program, until her death at age forty-one.

As for the rest of the space chimps and their progeny, rather than being given some measure of dignity in their later years, they would instead become subjects for various research projects. Some were used for seat belt testing—on occasion serving as what amounted to crash test dummies—subjected to violent rides in deceleration sleds. Many more were assigned to disease studies, being injected with everything from hepatitis to syphilis to malaria, and suffering dozens of so-called anesthetic "knock downs" in order to perform biopsies on their livers. Added to that were heart catheterizations, bone marrow retrieval, transplants, and motion sickness studies.

Indeed, over time the Air Force began leasing out more and more of the space chimps to laboratories; and starting in 1994, many ended up at the Coulston Foundation lab. There, in addition to the usual doses of disease agents, which eventually included HIV, the chimpanzees were also exposed to powerful carcinogens, ranging from insecticides to the gas additive benzene (which causes bone marrow failure), as well as to toxic industrial solvents like trichloroethylene. Primate scientist Roger Fouts, author of the celebrated book *Next of Kin: My Conversations with Chimpanzees*, recalls that he was once told of a protocol in which "chimps had their teeth bashed out so that dental students could practice reconstructive surgery on them."

With a creature as intelligent and as psychologically sophisticated as a chimpanzee, it's easy to imagine the kind of primal anxiety that would be ignited simply from the fear of physical harm. (Many of those who were finally rescued from the lab would for the rest of their lives display an abject terror of syringes.) Making matters worse was the fact that chimps at Coulston, like those at certain other biomedical labs, were cut off from the kind of basic amenities that would've helped ease their distress. With the exception of infants raised in a nursery, most of the lab chimps at Coulston lacked any sort of opportunity for playful engagement. There

were no blocks or toy trucks or hats or sunglasses or food retrieval puzzles or magazines or any of a dozen other things chimpanzees take great delight in. They often lacked even blankets, which sanctuaries routinely use to satisfy the strong desire chimps have to make nests, folding and twisting and rearranging the material with great creativity. Most troubling of all, though, was the frequent long-term isolation. Their lonely, dreary existence, which some chimps endured for decades, routinely led to severe depression, even psychosis.

AS FOR THE REST OF THE SPACE CHIMPS AND THEIR PROGENY, RATHER THAN BEING GIVEN SOME MEASURE OF DIGNITY IN THEIR LATER YEARS, THEY WOULD INSTEAD BECOME SUBJECTS FOR VARIOUS RESEARCH PROJECTS.

What was hardest for Carole Noon and other primate scientists to forgive, though, was the fact that all this was happening at a time when our understanding of the complex emotional and social life of chimps was gaining widespread acceptance,

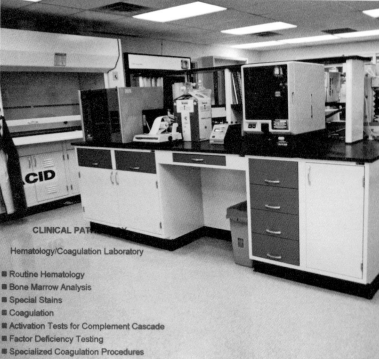

CLINICAL PAT...

Hematology/Coagulation Laboratory

■ Routine Hematology
■ Bone Marrow Analysis
■ Special Stains
■ Coagulation
■ Activation Tests for Complement Cascade
■ Factor Deficiency Testing
■ Specialized Coagulation Procedures

thanks in large part to the work of researchers like Jane Goodall. Well before the Air Force chimps landed at biomedical labs like Coulston, we knew, without a doubt, that they possessed an extraordinary range of emotional capacity, showing contentment, joy, anticipation and laughter, as well as fear, anxiety, and anger. There was no longer any question about chimps being highly intelligent. Indeed for anyone who cared to look, they routinely showed cognitive abilities that for much of history had been assumed to be the sole province of humans. They were considered capable of high levels of reasoned thought, able to link symbols with the objects they pointed to. And, as Jane Goodall pointed out, chimps showed "a capacity for intentional communication," which referred to a type of sharing that depends on understanding the motives of those you're communicating with.

Yet, when it came to providing for their general welfare, all this knowledge too often counted for nothing. While researchers routinely touted chimpanzees as perfect test subjects based on how incredibly similar they were to humans—sharing all but a tiny fraction of our own genetic material—those same researchers were often blind to the parts of that similarity having to do with emotional and psychological well being. As Dr. Noon told an interviewer years later, "With all this information, [the Air Force] was still prepared to throw these chimps away. That their conception of chimps hadn't evolved one iota in forty years, boggles my mind."

DESPITE HAVING AT ONE POINT ESTABLISHED AN
ACTIVE BREEDING PROGRAM AMONG THEIR CAPTIVE
CHIMPS—AND IN THE PROCESS MORE THAN DOUBLING
THEIR POPULATION—BY THE 1990s THE AIR FORCE WAS
SHOWING CLEAR SIGNS OF WANTING TO BE OUT OF
THE CHIMPANZEE BUSINESS ALTOGETHER. The first
attempt to be rid of their primate heroes was by
means of least resistance, involving a plan to simply
transfer ownership of any chimps in biomedical
studies to the various research institutions that
leased them. Some of those facilities, including
the Centers for Disease Control and Prevention
(CDC) in Atlanta, told the Air Force "thanks, but no
thanks." Then, in May of 1995, a bill was introduced
in the House of Representatives—a bill having to do
with construction on military bases—that contained

a bizarre provision authorizing the Secretary of the
Air Force to convey to the Coulston Foundation
"at no cost, all right title and interest of the United
States in all or part of the Advanced Primate
Research Biocontainment Facility at Holloman Air
Force Base, and ownership of the colony of Air
Force-owned chimpanzees used in connection
with research at the laboratory."

It was a noteworthy blunder. That very same year,
in a rare action by the Department of Agriculture, the
Coulston Foundation had been fined $40,000 for,
among other things, violations of the Animal Welfare
Act. The infractions included the brutal deaths
of three chimpanzees from heat stroke, caused
by employees placing space heaters in one of the
caged areas and then not bothering to check them,

raising temperatures to well over a hundred degrees. All efforts by primate researchers, including Jane Goodall, to actually visit the Coulston Foundation lab and make recommendations for improving the conditions there were firmly denied. Still, thanks to a small avalanche of letters and phone calls by Goodall and others to members of the House Committee on Homeland Security, the provision in the House bill to transfer Air Force chimps to the Coulston Foundation lab was finally removed.

The divesture would instead be accomplished by means of a formal request for proposals (RFP), which was essentially an invitation to interested parties to submit plans for the chimps' continued care. The goal of the divesture, as Air Force Captain Renee Richardson described it, was "to ensure that the chimpanzees [were] transferred only to a responsible recipient who [could] provide for [their] welfare." At odds with that idea, though—and this was a big red flag for Carole Noon and her fellow primatologists—was a declaration by the Air Force that they would show no preference among bidders between those seeking sanctuary for the chimps, and those intending to continue using them for experimentation. Most disease research requires chimps to be not only isolated in single cages, but typically even limits their ability to spend time in outdoor enclosures. Understandably, such conditions were at odds with the whole idea of "future care and welfare."

Despite public assurances that chimp welfare was the Air Force's major concern in chimp divestiture, in truth the military considered their chim-

BELOW *One of the residents of the Fauna Foundation chimpanzee sanctuary in Canada. Gloria Grow and Dr. Richard Allan started the organization in 1997.*

RIGHT *The Fauna Foundation.*

panzees surplus materials, to be discarded in the most efficient, least-expensive way possible. As the officer in charge of the divestment put it in an interview with the Wall Street Journal, "Chimps—right, wrong or otherwise—are basically personal property. They're like a piece of equipment."

The fire was lit, and Carole, with a group of fellow chimpanzee advocates—including primatologists Jane Goodall and Roger Fouts, along with consultant Lori Raab and infectious disease specialist Fred Prince—came together to hatch a plan. Carole was chosen to coordinate the effort, her work to be funded in part with money from the Doris Day

Animal League. "Over time Carole became kind of our alpha leader," recalls Gloria Grow, founder of the chimp sanctuary Fauna Foundation. "When we were talking about a strategy or some problem we were having, as often as not we'd ask ourselves 'What would Carole do? What would Carole think?' We didn't do that because we were submissive. We did it because she had this vast amount of knowledge, this way of thinking that was extremely valuable to our efforts."

There were tough decisions to make right from the start, including whether the group should build a new sanctuary or simply create a federation out of existing sanctuaries. On one hand, places already up and running had the advantage of established track records. What's more, it would likely be easier to move HIV-positive and hepatitis-positive chimps into existing sanctuaries than into a new one. (Early on, Carole Noon was told by a state resource agency in Florida that no county in the state would knowingly allow the building of a facility to house infected chimpanzees; then, to her astonishment, the same agency suggested it was probably best to just move the chimps in and tell the community about it later.)

But one big problem of using existing sanctuaries was the fact that many of them were already filled. Placing more than a hundred new residents from the Air Force would be difficult, requiring an estimated half a million dollars for every dozen chimps a sanctuary acquired. The federation model might also prove troublesome when it came to matters of quality control. But in the end, the working group also came to believe that a new facility, designed specifically for the Air Force chimps, might more fully excite the public. And that, in turn, might excite their financial support.

There were plenty of other tricky matters to still sort out. "I wanted the support of the humane community," Carole later recalled, "but I also needed to be taken seriously by the Air Force." She put together a board of directors made up of people with impeccable scientific credentials, who had "a proven track record of putting the best interest of chimpanzees first," but who key humane groups would feel comfortable rallying behind.

In late 1997 and early 1998, armed with an open letter of commitment from Jane Goodall, Carole made four trips to Washington, DC, to meet with animal welfare groups, including the Humane Society of the United States (HSUS) and the American Society for the Prevention of Cruelty to Animals (ASPCA). She laid out the vision for the chimp sanctuary, explained why their help was critical to the task, then presented both a budget and architectural plans, the latter having been provided free of charge by a firm in El Paso. At that time the annual collective resources of the groups she met with was about $170 million; Carole set a

private goal of trying to walk away with about three million dollars in contributions—"enough to put me over the laugh level with the bid," as she described it. In the end, she took away only $100,000 in cash and $250,000 in pledges.

It wasn't exactly the hot start she was hoping for. A key criteria set by the Air Force for potential recipients was going to be financial stability, and her current bank account of about $350,000 was a long way from that. Carole made an educated guess that the Air Force would expect bidders to spend ten to fifteen dollars a day on each chimp across his or her entire lifetime; those per-diem costs alone would amount to more than six million dollars. Still, she and her colleagues—having formed a group with the rather chewy name of the Institute for Captive Chimpanzee Care and Well-Being—put their heads down and plowed ahead.

FOR THOSE WHO HOPED TO PROVIDE THE AIR FORCE CHIMPS WITH A DIGNIFIED RETIREMENT, THINGS WEREN'T GOING SO WELL. BEYOND THE CHALLENGE OF RAISING THE MILLIONS OF DOLLARS NEEDED TO BECOME A VIABLE ALTERNATIVE TO A PLACE LIKE COULSTON, the Institute, now renamed the Center for Captive Chimpanzee Care (CCCC) and other bidders were routinely stymied by the Air Force when they sought detailed information about the chimps' social and medical status. For example, countless attempts were made to get information about which chimps had been infected with diseases, and if so, with what diseases. But those efforts went nowhere. And that was an enormous stumbling block for anyone trying to draft plans for lifelong care.

In November of 1997 the Air Force offered a tour of the Holloman Base for prospective bidders, allowing them to see the chimps and related facilities included in the divestment. This tour was filmed and turned into a video, allowing those who couldn't attend to still have a chance to see the offerings. Though one might expect such a film to be lackluster, especially given the official view of the transaction as nothing but a divesture of property, there was a bleakness to it, a lack of feeling that seemed utterly bizarre. Against a backdrop of tinny marimba music—the kind of soulless, meandering tunes reminiscent of a grade school safety film from the 1960s— the potential bidders were shepherded onto a bus and driven into the desert past clusters of bleak, windowless buildings. Tour leader Howard Moffitt held fast to a clipboard in his hand, scanning notes while describing the assets: "Building 1267, built in 1957 as a primate housing facility. 2,880 square feet. Building 1204, which served as a primate lab." Then buildings 1269 and 1264 and on and on, with the vast majority of the structures now being used as glorified storage sheds. Against the rear wall of one of the old primate housing facilities the camera showed a line of empty outdoor cages, surrounded by barbed wire and razor fencing. It was a gruesome, dismal-looking world—a cross between a prison labor camp and a huddle of atomic bomb shelters.

In the next scene of the movie, Denver Marlow from the Air Force Surgeon General's Office came

LEFT *Ham before his historic flight. The chimpanzees from the Coulston Foundation were mixed up with those from Holloman Air Force Base, so the government couldn't say for sure which chimpanzees were up for bidding.*

aboard the bus to talk to the bidders about the actual Air Force chimpanzees, 114 of which are on site—the rest being out on loan to various biomedical labs. But the Air Force chimps were mixed in with those owned by the Coulston Foundation, making it impossible to sort out who was who. Most of the chimps the group observed were being housed in groups, with access to outdoor runs for exercise. What wasn't shown were those living alone, isolated in cages because of their active status in various disease studies. Marlow wasn't able to answer questions about how long they had been isolated, what they had been infected with, or the duration of the various research trials.

This persistent lack of information would soon become troubling even to Congress. In March of 1998, thirty-seven Congressmen wrote a letter to the Air Force captain in charge of divestment, urging more cooperation. "The inability of potential bidders to get background information is particularly troubling," the letter read, "when it is noted that the only potential bidder with such access is …the Coulston Foundation." Two months later they sent another letter, this time to Secretary of Defense William Cohen. Besides complaining about the lack of medical histories, the legislators impressed on Secretary Cohen that this divesture was about something more than used equipment: "The USAF has characterized the chimpanzees' divesture as it would that of old tanks, planes or ammunition," they said. "However, this is not the case in the minds of the American public, many of whom feel a certain debt to the Air Force chimpanzees for their contribution to our country's space program. The United States Congress has a moral obligation to ensure that their divestiture, which we authorized, is truly open and fair so that they have a chance at retirement."

WHAT WASN'T SHOWN WERE THOSE CHIMPS LIVING ALONE, ISOLATED IN CAGES BECAUSE OF THEIR ACTIVE STATUS IN DISEASE STUDIES.

Chimpanzee advocates, meanwhile, were making much the same point to anyone who would listen. Along the way they were joined by former astronauts Buzz Aldrin, James Lovell, Edgar Mitchell, Scott Carpenter, Michael Collins, Charles "Pete" Conrad, Jr., Robert Crippen, Gerald Carr, Eugene Cernan, Gordon Cooper, "Walt" Cunningham, Richard Gordon, Jack Lousma, and James McDivitt. In May of 1998, this group of men signed off on a letter to the military encouraging them to "acknowledge and appreciate the enormous debt we owe the space chimpanzees, whose contribution to our country began when they were taken from their homes in Africa." Those chimps and their descendents, they continued, had served the country in a great many ways. It was now "time to repay this debt by giving these veterans the peaceful and permanent retirement they deserve."

TO AN INCREASING NUMBER OF PRIMATOLOGISTS AND ANIMAL WELFARE ADVOCATES, THERE WAS A GROWING SENSE THAT THE GAME WAS RIGGED IN THE COULSTON FOUNDATION'S FAVOR. Such thoughts become more troubling still when in March of 1998, Coulston was again cited for violations of the Animal Welfare Act. This time the infractions included lapses that led to the death of a chimpanzee who'd been anesthetized not in isolation, as was standard protocol, but in a group of other chimps; while sedated another chimp apparently stood on his neck, suffocating him. Still another Coulston chimp, Echo, had been operated on for a broken arm, apparently by inexperienced veterinarians who left him alone after the procedure, and therefore weren't around to notice when he went into shock and died.

But Fred Coulston wasn't going away. In the wake of a growing mountain of bad press, company managers Ron Couch and Don McKinney typed

up an internal memo to employees, letting them know in no uncertain terms that the company was "aggressively pursuing" the contract for the government chimps, "and INTENDS TO WIN THE RFP." They also warned against having any contact with outside entities, claiming the need for loyalty if Coulston was to "persevere during times of attacks on the Foundation by outside sources." This latter point was made again two days later in a memo from Fred Coulston himself, who cautioned employees about breeching confidentiality about "contracts, grant proposals, responses to an RFP, secret processes, techniques, formulae, procedures, pricing formulae, records, memorandums, drawings, customer relation methods, and any other information deemed confidential by the Board of Directors."

Locked in fighting mode, Fred Coulston, with great bravado, began using the press to caution the public about giving the Air Force chimps to organizations not bound by the Animal Welfare Act. "You can't give them to just anyone," he warned. Defending his lab at every turn, as often as not he blamed his troubles on an animal welfare group based in California called In Defense of Animals, which included the tenacious Eric Kleiman. "We take really good care of these animals," Coulston told an Alamogordo newspaper reporter. "We do everything possible to see to their comfort and safety."

As it happened, the same media that Fred Coulston would, by turns, either shun or court favor with, was possibly a little more interested in chimpanzees than usual due to a recent report by the Institute of Laboratory Animal Resources at the National Research Council, an operating arm of the National Academy of Sciences. Based on more than a year of work by nine primate experts, the re-

port stated in no uncertain terms that while chimps may have a role in research, the similarity of chimps to humans "distinguishes them in substantial ways from other laboratory animals, and implies a moral responsibility for their long-term care." The report went on to address what had become an excess of research chimpanzees in the country, much of it the result of a National Institutes of Health (NIH) breeding program started in 1986, in large part due to the mistaken notion that chimps would be ideal test subjects for AIDS research. When this didn't prove to be the case (chimps infected with the human immunodeficiency virus, or HIV, don't go on to develop AIDS), the NIH was suddenly stuck with having far more chimpanzees than researchers required. The scientists behind the report called for a five-year moratorium on chimp breeding, and at the same time, said euthanasia should not be used as a means of reducing the population. They further called on

NIH to provide a cohesive management program for chimps, part of which would involve the eventual development of sanctuaries to house lab chimpanzees once they were retired from research.

At the same time, various primate advocates around the country were working night and day to make their appeal for sanctuary resonate with average Americans, reminding them at every opportunity how special chimps really were. Some would end up pointing yet again to the famous Washoe, a former space program chimp from Africa who, in 1967, went from a dismal future at Holloman Air Force Base to doing a series of language studies with researchers Alex Gardener, Beatrix Gardener, and Roger Fouts. While past efforts to teach chimps to literally speak had failed (they lack the vocal equipment to sound out words), Fouts and the Gardeners decided to try sign language instead. Unlike the majority

RON

RON, WHO USED TO LIVE ALONE IN THE DUNGEON, WOULD BE SURROUNDED BY HUMANS WHO LOVED HIM, A TICKET TO FLORIDA IN HIS POCKET.

BEING A BIG GUY ISN'T EASY, EVEN WHEN YOU'RE A REALLY NICE BIG GUY. RON COULD'VE TOLD YOU THAT. TO MAKE HIS CASE HE MIGHT'VE THOUGHT BACK TO 2004—AFTER SAVE THE CHIMPS HAD TAKEN OVER THE OLD COULSTON LAB IN NEW MEXICO— WHEN HE WAS INTRODUCED TO TWO 10 YEAR-OLD MALES NAMED LAYNE AND GARTH. Layne met Ron first, and not surprisingly, was completely taken aback by his size; still, Layne gave Ron a chance, working through the hard stuff of just getting used to being around somebody that big. Pretty soon the two were friends, playing and grooming each other at every chance.

Garth was another story. Try as he might he just couldn't get over Ron's size; no matter how many times Ron tried to be friends, Garth remained terrified. Not knowing what else to do Ron finally took Layne by one hand and started to follow Garth around, all the while holding his other hand out to his frightened new neighbor. "He was saying," mused Carole, "'See, Garth, your friend Layne here isn't afraid of me. I just know we can all be friends!'" And it

worked. Garth swallowed hard and accepted the offer, and soon all three were living together. Which left many of the caregivers thinking that if you're going to be big, it's also helpful to be smart.

Still, all the extra effort a big guy has to exert in order to fit in can sometimes take its toll. By the time Ron's full group had been assembled he'd become reserved, refusing— along with another chimp named Thoto—to even leave his cage for cleaning. "I think they were scared," says Mikey, who was one of Ron's primary caregivers at the time. Ron just didn't know what was coming next, Mikey speculates— didn't know what the next chimp meeting would look like, and that was stressing him out. Mikey's assessment may have been on the mark, given that once the group settled in and stabilized, Ron started moving to and from his cage again during cleaning with no problems.

Though there are no records of Ron's early years, estimates put his birthday somewhere around 1973. He was probably involved in biomedical research as a youngster, though the first evidence of his life in the labs

comes from June, 1987, when he was given a physical at the Laboratory for Experimental Medicine and Surgery in Primates (LEMSIP), north of New York City. Living alone in a suspended five-by-five-by-seven-foot cage—an especially harsh circumstance given his size, at over 140 pounds—in the course of his nine years at LEMSIP he would be anesthetized with ketamine more than a hundred times, often for prolonged periods. When LEMSIP finally

HE WOULD MAKE IT, OF COURSE, BECAUSE ONE WAY OR ANOTHER RON HAD A KNACK FOR MAKING IT.

closed in the late 1990's, Ron was sent to the Coulston lab in Alamogordo.

After arriving in New Mexico he was transported again—this time to the nearby primate lab on Holloman Air Force Base—assigned to a research study that led to sixteen more anesthetizations over a five week period. In 1998 he was ferried yet again to Holloman for a so-called Spinal Dynamics study, in which one of his healthy cervical discs was removed and replaced with a prosthetic; six months later the prosthetic was surgically removed. Incredibly, Ron received no pain medication for that surgery, given only a token amount of ibuprofen eight days after the operation.

Then in August of 2004—nearly two years after Save the Chimps took over the Coulston lab—Ron was hit with major health problems. He started retaining water, and after a couple days his eyes were puffy and his stomach and scrotum badly swelled. Despite no clear history of cardiac problems (an abnormal echocardiogram in 1997 had been dismissed as being caused by anesthetic), Dr. Jocelyn Bezner, Save the Chimps' veterinarian, suspected this was the source of his problems. Her immediate concern was whether or not fluid had built up around his heart; if so, it would have to be drained, which meant a call to a cardiac specialist to arrange an ultrasound. Carole was traveling during all this, and as the treatment proceeded Jen Feuerstein—Carole's right-hand woman in New Mexico—was keeping her posted by phone. At one point she called Carole with news: Ron's heart had been failing, all right. And then it stopped beating altogether, though Dr. Bezner was able to bring him back. This happened another time, and then it happened still again. In all he would die three times that day, and each time Dr. Bezner brought him back. And even that wasn't the end of it. Ron would actually die a fourth time, though somehow, without medicine, he managed to bring himself back.

"I didn't know if Ron would be alive when I got back," Carole wrote, "but I had a good idea of what I would find either way. Ron, who used to live alone in the dungeon, would be surrounded by humans who loved him, his good dinner waiting on the food cart, his new chimp family wondering where he was and a ticket to Florida in his pocket."

Several days after the treatment Ron returned to his family. The puffiness and swelling were gone, and he was responding well to his heart medicine. Maybe one of the best signs he was feeling better was his loud complaints about having to pick carrots out of his rice casserole. Still, as a result of his fragile condition Ron was now on a high priority list

to get to Florida. And by the following spring he was there, arriving in May with his buddy Thoto, the chimp who'd also refused to leave his cage for cleaning. On being released to their island at Save the Chimps, though, while Thoto was fearless, making a fast beeline for the farthest corner of the island, Ron was timid, staying on the cement patio, not at all sure about that stuff called grass. But he would make it, of course, because one way or another Ron had a knack for making it. In 2007 the big guy, along with a female chimp named April, served as perfect surrogate parents for a blustery little baby chimp named Melody.

Ron passed away from heart failure in October, 2011— six good years after using that ticket to Florida Carole once imagined him having in his pocket.

OPPOSITE *Ron's friend, Thoto, shown here with a blanket on his back, helped to show Ron the joys of island life.*

BELOW *Dr. Jocelyn Bezner, the veterinarian at Save the Chimps, with Carole.*

CHAPTER 03

Against All Odds

I F CAROLE NOON'S TENACITY CAN BE SAID TO HAVE HAD A BLOOMING SEASON, IT WAS IN 1998, WHEN SHE MARRIED IT WITH UNREASONABLE OPTIMISM AND PUT IN A BID FOR 141 AIR FORCE CHIMPANZEES—FORMER SPACE RACE HEROES WHO WERE NOW CONSIDERED "SURPLUS MATERIAL." What's more, she did so without even having an established facility in which to place them, though she and her colleagues were moving as fast as possible in that direction. At the time, as she later recalled, "Save the Chimps had $150,000 in cash, and was pretty much nothing more than a good idea." Thus, in truth, no one, least of all Carole, was much surprised when the Air Force denied her bid. "That's what they should've done," she confessed.

Yet it soon became obvious that there was method behind her madness. While she may not have ended up with any chimps, her organization, due to the fact that it had been a participant in the proposal process, and for that reason only, now had legal standing to sue the Air Force for violating the stated goals of its own request for proposals. And that's when the tenacious part of Carole, along with perhaps just the right dose of naivety and extraordinary luck, started showing itself for real. She got on the telephone and started calling legal firms—more than a dozen—but all she came away with was

ABOVE *Nadia.*

OPPOSITE *Carole Noon giving one of the chimpanzees formula in a bottle. The staff at Save the Chimps often administer vitamins or medicine mixed in a small amount of juice.*

ABOVE LEFT *Chimps at the Alamogordo facilities.*

ABOVE RIGHT *Esmerelda.*

sobering news about what a lawsuit like that would cost. Frustrated, she finally called a lawyer friend of Jane Goodall's, who suggested the firm of Spriggs & Hollinsworth in Washington, DC.

As Carol recounted: "I got on the phone and I told my little tale, you know—the Air Force just gave some chimps to a lab, blah blah blah—and they put me on the phone with Mr. Spriggs himself. And when I told him my story, luckily he said, 'I saw something about that this morning on Good Morning America.'" To Carole's amazement, Spriggs said he would take the case. Furthermore, he would take it pro bono. A year or so later Carole went to DC to meet with Bill in person, finding herself walking into a "high-fallutin' law firm in a posh downtown Washington office building. You get off the elevator, they offer you coffee, they offer you bottled water. If I had known where I was calling, I never would've had the nerve."

THE TASK OF ACTUALLY PICKING WHICH OF THE AIR FORCE CHIMPS WOULD COME TO THE SANCTUARY IN FLORIDA FELL TO THEIR CURRENT CARETAKERS—THE STAFF AT THE COULSTON FOUNDATION LAB. Their choices made for an odd group. Of the seven males chosen, five were born in Africa and over forty years old, and then there was a twenty-two-year-old named Waylon (a fellow with little social experience, but a huge heart), and a big, testosterone-filled eleven-year-old, a little short on common sense, named Garfield. The females, on the other hand, were spread out more evenly as far as ages were concerned, ranging from a nine-year-old to a forty-year-old. Despite numerous attempts by Carole to figure out the rationale used to make the selections, none of the employees at Coulston seemed to have any clue. Which may mean there was no reasoning behind it at all.

Still, it was official. It was happening. Better times were on the way for Hanzie, Emory, Faith, Waylon, Kendra, Debbie, Phyllis, Marty, and Gromek; for Wes, Garfield, Emily, Gogi, Tammy, Lil' Mini, Amy, Hannah, Jennifer, Daisy, Dana, and Liza.

Years later, late one fall night in 2006, in an email note to Jon Stryker, Carole found herself in a mood to reminisce about some of the highlights of her life—"peak moments," as she called them. She mentioned falling in love for the first time with Michael, who she would end up being married to for ten years. She listed her time in Africa at Chimfunshi as well, when Milla, the rescued chimpanzee, took hold of Carole's hand and led her to the nest she'd made, so happy with her newfound freedom that it took a week before she even came inside again. She mentioned, too, the first time she was ever published, in a local Cincinnati newspaper. But among her very favorite peak experiences, she told Jon, was "us at the dining room table in Palm Beach a thousand years ago. I said if you want to help the Air Force chimps, it is now or never—and you said, 'I want to help.'"

ABOVE *Amy, Hannah, and Garfield, three of the original Air Force chimpanzees.*

In truth, if the Air Force suit hadn't worked out Carole had a "Plan B," which was to go back to work with Sheila and David Siddle again at their magnificent Chimfunshi sanctuary in Zambia. One way or another, she was going to be with chimpanzees. But with the awarding of those twenty-one Air Force chimps, along with the pledge from Jon Stryker to help prepare and maintain a place for them, suddenly her long-held vision of a chimp sanctuary was a reality. And that unleashed a frenzy of effort that would be hard to imagine a lesser person being able to endure.

Jon Stryker
THE ESSENTIAL COMPANION

THE LAWSUIT AGAINST THE AIR FORCE WORE ON, MONTH AFTER MONTH, WITH CAROLE CONTINUING TO HOPE FOR SOME KIND OF SETTLEMENT. But after a year of negotiations led by her attorneys at Spriggs & Hollinsworth, the Air Force turned away, telling her she'd have to take them to court. And while she was perfectly willing to go to that next level, the fact was that even if she won the lawsuit, finances remained a thorny problem. Not only were chimps incredibly expensive to care for, but there was the not inconsequential matter of actually building a sanctuary. At one point she wrote to the various people who'd already made donations to the effort—about $150,000 in total—telling them, "I've got momentum now, but [if you'd prefer] I'll send you your money back. Or, you can keep it invested in me and let me move forward and see where I can go." Not a single person or group backed out.

Still, little could she have imagined that an unexpected angel—or, at the very least, a king-sized blessing—was about to land in her lap in the form of a generous philanthropist named Jon Stryker. Founder of the Arcus Foundation, Stryker, in the years that followed would become not just a critical supporter of the Save the Chimps effort, but also one of Carole's dearest friends and closest confidants. Appropriately, their relationship started in somewhat miraculous fashion.

"One day my nine-year-old daughter and I were on the Internet," recalls Stryker. "Actually, we were on a Barbie

website." Then his daughter suggested they do a search for Jane Goodall. The first thing to show up on their Internet search was Carole Noon and her Center for Captive Chimpanzee Care (later known as Save the Chimps), of which Jane Goodall was a part, likely because of all the media attention Carole had been getting about the Air Force chimps. They clicked on the website and started reading about Carole, including her work in Africa. Jon owned a house in Palm Beach, which as it turned out was only about fifteen miles away from where Carole was living. He picked up the phone and called her, explaining that he and his daughter were interested in her project, and suggesting they get together sometime to talk about the possibilities.

While it's certainly striking that Carole and Jon would be brought together by a young girl searching the Internet, the fact that Stryker's daughter was interested in primates in the first place is less mysterious. Jon himself had long been a lover of animals, especially monkeys and the great apes, going all the way back to when he was five years old. Montages of primates adorned the walls of his boyhood bedroom: "When I was five I had a white teddy bear and

ended up naming it Snowflake, after an albino gorilla I'd seen on a National Geographic cover."

As a boy Jon would even go on to have a pet monkey for a time, which he called Nicky, who was bought at a mall pet store—a somewhat miraculous turn of events, considering his mother had long insisted that she would never, ever have a monkey living in her house. After a year with Nicky, though, the problem of having an energetic primate as a pet became all too clear, and in the end it led Jon to start writing letters in an attempt to find another home for his little friend.

"The director of the Lincoln Park Children's Zoo wrote back and said they would take him," recalled Stryker. To this day that response seems incredible to him, given that this particular zoo, like so many others in modern times,

actually had a policy against taking these sorts of pets. "I was really lucky," he admits. "Normally it's a tragic ending for pet monkeys. They end up in labs, or at some sort of awful zoo, or as part of a breeding colony. Of course that also applies to pet chimps. They go from being nurtured, practically treated as human children, and then they get unmanageable so they get sent to some sort of terrible facility. Even in the best circumstances, when they end up at a sanctuary, they have a really hard time figuring out how to be a chimp."

As Jon grew older he became fascinated in particular with the monkeys of South America, and before heading off to college to study biology he joined an Earthwatch Institute project, spending three weeks with scientists tracking a family of monkeys through the jungles of Peru.

This fascination with primates never went away. "Before we ever met Carole, my daughter and I had toyed with the idea of one day starting a monkey sanctuary—someplace for pet monkeys like the one I had who were in need of homes. When we heard about what Carole was doing for chimpanzees, it seemed to fit well into that dream."

Jon recalls being impressed right away with not only how knowledgeable Carole was, but also how passionate: "At the same time she was always very grounded, never putting on airs." The first time they actually talked face to face was

"CAROLE WASN'T JUST TENACIOUS, SHE WAS ABSOLUTELY TIRELESS— A WOMAN OF SUCH DRIVE IT WAS HARD NOT TO BE PULLED INTO THE MISSION."

OPPOSITE LEFT *Jeannie peers through the door to her new home. In her hand is a stuffed animal.*

OPPOSITE AND LEFT *Mandy and Garfield.*

at Jon's house in Palm Beach, the two of them sitting in the backyard discussing chimps, with Carole even offering up a couple of "pant hoot" greetings and mimicking various other chimp behaviors. By the end of that first meeting, she and Jon were already on their way to becoming good friends.

Carole's second trip to Jon's house came after she'd gotten word that negotiations with the Air Force had broken down. "I went to him and said, 'If you want to help, now would be the time.' He told me he was willing to give $750,000 to buy land for a sanctuary, then another two million dollars as a matching grant to build the actual facility. When I got up off the floor, I called the lawyer and

said, 'We'd like to settle out of court.' As a result of Jon's pledge, I was no longer a long shot." Following a meeting on primate welfare in Washington that Jon helped arrange with Michigan Senator Carl Levin, Carole got word that she'd been awarded twenty-one of the Air Force chimps. Some have suggested, only half-jokingly, that Carole simply wore the Air Force down.

"Without Jon," she explained later, "I would've been nothing but a good idea. Save the Chimps was pretty much me at my desk in Boynton Beach with a killer website and a wonderful pro bono law team."

WHEN IT CAME TO CHOOSING A LOCATION FOR THE SAVE THE CHIMPS SANCTUARY, THERE WERE LOTS OF POSSIBILITIES, WARM WEATHER BEING ONE OF THE PRIMARY CONDITIONS. But early on Jon spoke up and narrowed the search. "Carole was considering going to Texas," he says. "But I told her that if I was going to fund this thing I wanted to be nearby. I wanted it to be in Florida." And so the two new partners headed out across the southern reaches of the Sunshine State, looking for land. They began in Palm Beach County, close to where each was living at the time, but real estate was far too expensive. So they pushed north to Martin County. There were some fine possibilities there, but no one from the local governments seemed much inclined to lay down a welcome mat for them. "The county commissioners really wanted homes built on those lands," recalls Jon. "Either that, or to keep the land in agriculture." So, the two kept going, moving further north still. Then one day Jon got a call from Carole.

"'I think I've found the place," she said, describing a 150-acre tract of land in an abandoned orange grove west of the town of Fort Pierce. The location was good. The price was manageable. And unlike the neighboring counties to the south, the commissioners of St. Lucie County saw the chimp sanctuary as an opportunity—a logical extension even, for the kind of scientific and environmental research facilities they'd been successfully courting for years.

Doug Coward was a county commissioner in St. Lucie County at the time, and he remembers well his first meeting with Carole Noon. He'd gotten a call ahead of time from a land use planner named

OPPOSITE *An aerial view of Save the Chimps. The different islands can be clearly seen. Each one can be accessed from the main grounds by a thin strip of land.*

ABOVE *Garfield exploring his island for the first time.*

Morris Crady, whom Jon and Carole had hired to help scout locations; Morris described the idea to the commissioner, and Coward said he'd be interested in hearing more about it.

"Two hours later," Coward recalls, "Carole was in my office laying out her vision. She wasn't just tenacious. She was absolutely tireless—a woman of such drive it was hard not to be pulled into the mission." During this initial meeting a couple of other commissioners happened to be in the building, so

"WHAT DOES ANYONE KNOW ABOUT BUILDING A CHIMP CITY? NO MODEL TO FOLLOW, NO ONE TO ASK."

would need to make building pads ready to erect the necessary offices, maintenance buildings, and shelter houses, and to build the first island. There were security systems and water treatment facilities and heating units and landscaping to design, a kitchen to build for food preparation, washers and dryers to buy and install, which would be used each day to clean the cloth blankets the chimps used as nesting material. The shelter houses especially required an extraordinary amount of forethought, including hundreds of decisions about the size and layout of the rooms and the placement of doors—all of which was essential to the task of making introductions, as well as for providing safe escape paths for chimps who weren't getting along.

There were safety protocols to develop, as well as plans for cleaning, feeding, and veterinary treatment. There was staff to train, only a few of whom had any previous experience, a board of directors to keep informed, and the media to deal with. "What does anybody know about building a chimp city?" Carole asked in a letter to a colleague. "No model to follow, no one to ask—all best guesses."

Underneath the hustle and bustle was a strong sense of urgency, fueled by the fact that the twenty-one chimps Carole had been awarded through the lawsuit were to remain housed at the former Coulston Foundation lab until the Florida sanctuary was ready to receive them. But although not a day passed when she didn't feel anxious about that arrangement, she never veered away from trying to create a sanctuary that wasn't just functional, but beautiful.

A talented local site developer named Wayne had been teamed with an equally capable project manager, Jennie, and while there was nothing easy about the project, both were flexible enough to incorporate Carole's aesthetic concerns. Early on, for example, Carole made the decision to slow Wayne down a bit (and at the same time, begin paying him more) in order that he could clear around the various oaks and palms on the property when preparing the building pads, instead of simply cutting them down. Sometime later, one evening while staring at the site plans for the sanctuary, Carole was troubled by how brittle the triangle-shaped islands and square roads would end up looking, especially as seen from the air. So the next morning she called another meeting with Wayne, this time asking him what it would take to start sculpting the islands into more flowing, free-form shapes. They discussed the roads as well—wondering how they could be made less straight and rigid, a question that led the two of them to climb aboard a bulldozer and begin planning a route that would hug the thirty-three-acre lake, twisting and turning through the trees. Later on, when Wayne, Jennie, and Carole drove down the meandering road together for the first time, Carole described it as "almost a religious experience."

"Wayne is really getting into it," she wrote in her diary. "He's never been given aesthetic license before. Last week he called Jennie to ask her to move one of the buildings thirty feet to save a huge oak tree." It pleased Carole to no end that they were creating not just a functioning chimpanzee sanctuary, but what she liked to think of as one of the prettiest places in the state.

"THIS PROJECT IS BLESSED WITH JUST THE RIGHT PEOPLE AT JUST THE RIGHT TIME AND ALWAYS WITH SOME SPECIAL MAGIC. HOW ELSE DO YOU EXPLAIN THE WONDER OF IT ALL?"

While there was a long string of frustrations (setbacks with the water treatment facility alone nearly brought her to her knees), she always found plenty of reason to get up in the morning, after very little sleep, and start in again. "Guess what?" she wrote in her diary. "Chimpanzees will be moving in here. Monkey chow-eating chimps, chimps who lived alone or in small same sex groups, chimps who underwent research we can't even guess about. Yes, these very same rocking, poop smearing chimps without a future will be moving into this very upscale neighborhood to live on big islands in big groups with lots of other chimps. Like I've said since the early days, this project is blessed with just the right people at just the right time and always with some special magic. How else do you explain the wonder of it all?"

It was during the frenzy of construction when Jon Stryker saw firsthand how an extra layer of frustration was sometimes heaped on Carole because of her hard-driving, decisive personality. "A man who is fierce and strong is called a leader," says Stryker, "while a woman with those same qualities is called a witch." As an example, Stryker recalls the day he accompanied Carole to a metal fabrication shop to check out progress on the doors, locks, and other parts needed for the shelter houses: "We had engineers involved the whole way—shop drawings and all that. But when we went to the shop to check on the progress, we discovered the workers had changed the drawings. Carole confronted them, and they basically told her 'don't worry about it, honey—we know what we're doing.' It infuriated her, and she

confronted that sort of thing all the time." ("I know I can be bad," Carole wrote to Jon years later, referring to her frequent blustery behavior. "But sometimes you just have to speak your mind or your mind will explode. Kind of like a sneeze—hold it all in and try to muffle it—and there go your ear drums.")

Despite her reputation for being fierce, Carole cherished many of the people she came to work with on the project, both at Save the Chimps and elsewhere. Sometimes the bond was instant. In other cases it took a while to knock off the rough edges, as with her relationship with the long-time construction supervisor for the Florida sanctuary—a clever, dedicated man named Cliff. It would be no

exaggeration to say that in the early days Carole and Cliff detested one another. But over time, working side by side, each came to see the qualities of the other, appreciating the dependable intelligence, insight, and tenacity. They grew incredibly close, on many evenings sharing worries and outrages and jokes over cold beer and cigarettes. "When Carole was on her death bed," recalls one sanctuary volunteer, "she told us she'd made Cliff promise that he'd never leave this place, never leave the chimps." Cliff agreed. To this day he remains a vital part of Save the Chimps.

ABOVE *The roof will shield the chimps from the hot Florida sun.*

Getting to Know You
THE FINE ART OF SOCIALIZATION

I**T'S EASY TO STAND ON A SUN-SPLASHED MORNING AT SAVE THE CHIMPS IN FLORIDA, WATCHING CHIMPS CLIMBING ON THEIR ISLAND TOWERS AND RUSTLING FOR GOODIES HIDDEN FOR THEM IN THE GRASS,** crawling through tunnels or sprawled out on their backs staring into the sky, and assume that such contentment flows from the brilliance of the place itself. Much of it does. Sanctuary Director Jen Feuerstein and her incredible staff, along with veterinarian Jocelyn Bezner and her dedicated team, and scores of volunteers, continue to make this sanctuary everything it can be. But chimps are incredibly complex social creatures, and when in the wrong company, disagreements and fights can break out, some of which may prove serious, even deadly. Helping them reach a relaxed, satisfied state means providing a certain sense of stability, and that means giving them an honest-to-goodness sense of community.

This was the aspect of rescue foremost on Carole Noon's mind, beginning way back in Africa during her work with

> JUST LIKE HUMAN COMMUNITIES, CHIMP CLANS ARE MADE UP OF DYNAMIC, CHANGING RELATIONSHIPS.

Jane Goodall and with the Siddles at Chimfunshi. And if her initial quest to unearth some kind of formula for socialization was by her own conclusion an impossible task, the journey nonetheless left her well-versed in how to create conditions under which the chimps themselves could do the figuring. "Some adults are gentle and easy to introduce, and some four year olds are terrors," she said. Just like human communities, chimp clans are made up of dynamic, changing relationships. Friends today may be adversaries tomorrow, and—perhaps more commonly than in human communities—today's adversaries may wake up tomorrow and decide they're friends.

When a strong leader passes away someone else will rise up to take that position, and at that point the entire group might fall apart. Some chimps will take this one's side, others will support someone else, and all of a sudden everyone will be fighting all the time. For as long as Save the Chimps exists, there will be a constant need to adjust and sometimes relocate chimps to different families.

If you wanted to, say, introduce an adult female chimp to a group of adults, she'd first require her own protected cage to live in—an enclosure with a barred window or grill mesh to allow socializing on a limited basis. This socializing would usually begin with her meeting other chimps one at a time, and that will hopefully progress to her having limited interactions with pairs or small groups. (The record number of introductions in a single day, by the way, is five, though it is

rare for things to go that quickly.) What's more, given that group dynamics can change with each new addition, sometimes the staff at Save the Chimps can find themselves adding or removing individuals, which can be like starting over.

In the early weeks following the release of the Air Force chimps, Waylon was terribly reluctant to go out onto the island. But was it because being outside scared him, which would certainly be understandable, or was it because his new family scared him? To answer that question the staff moved him, along with Dana—just those two—to a new, recently constructed island, and then waited to see what would happen. On the first day Waylon never left the patio. On the second day, though, with no hesitation at all he headed out and started exploring the island, which he continued for several hours, unquestionably delighted. "We learned an important lesson," said Carole. "Waylon can explore an island if he likes the people he's exploring with."

For a group of chimps who've been living together for a long time, and are thus closely bonded with one another, introducing newcomers can require literally months of effort. Even infants, who on first glance would seem to offer no threat

at all to a stable group, are often first placed with an adult or older juvenile chimp, who serves as a kind of protector during the delicate days of meeting the larger group.

At Chimfunshi where Dr. Noon did much of her doctoral work, newcomers tended to arrive either individually or in pairs. Through the introduction process described above, they were formed into subgroups, which were then let out in shifts into a larger enclosure. Sometimes a particularly aggressive chimpanzee in a clan could be "softened up" a bit by bringing a fully adult male or very strong female into the group. In addition, it was common for alliances to form between two or three chimps who were being introduced to a larger group; that friendship could be a big help in easing their transition into the larger clan, allowing the newcomers to stand up to aggressive individuals who just didn't appreciate any changes being made to the roster.

Any way you cut it, we're talking about an awful lot of meetings. To form family groups out of the twenty-one Air Force chimps would require over four hundred introductions; the clan known as Rufus's group, meanwhile, consisting of twenty-five chimps, took more than five hundred. When Save the Chimps acquired the Coulston Foundation lab, everyone understood that getting the residents into functioning groups that could live well at the Florida sanctuary would take years to complete. Even in natural conditions in the wilds of Africa, where it's most often a female in estrus who joins an already established group, that joining isn't always easy.

The chaos that occasionally erupts when two chimps, or two groups of chimps, are brought together for the first time can leave the casual observer ducking for cover. The shrieking alone can be startling, made worse by the fact any chimps watching nearby will feel compelled to add their own shouting to the chorus. Sometimes wrestling matches erupt, with chimps rolling around on the floor in a blur, black hair flying. At some zoos, staff often have fire hoses at the ready to separate the fighters, turning on the water at the first signs of trouble. While Save the Chimps had hoses too,

Dr. Noon considered them a last resort, pointing out that even fights that looked terrible often yielded only minor cuts and scrapes to the players. She was also a fan of using loud noises to break up fights—an air horn, for instance—a strategy she gained at Chimfunshi after seeing squabbling chimps halted in their tracks by the sound of a backfiring car. Most of all, though, she believed that introduction buildings should have plenty of escape routes, giving easy outs to any chimps who've had enough.

It's worth noting that when two chimpanzees have a routine fight—maybe someone steals an orange from another, or in some way hurts their feelings—they get offended, and when they're offended they usually complain. What they want most is an apology from the offender, some kind of admission of guilt, at least an acknowledgement that the other chimp behaved badly. In absence of such good manners being offered up, more often than not a chimp will scream with displeasure. "If Amy steals Tammy's apple at lunch, it is bad," said Carole, "but if Amy acknowledges the theft, instead of pretending it never happened, that helps. A small look of remorse also might do. Even better is a pat on the back, which is reassurance among family members that says, 'I don't know what came over me and I'm sorry.'" Unlike some humans, chimps can be quick to forgive.

One of the most significant challenges Carole made to existing beliefs about chimpanzee socialization was the long-held notion that only youngsters could be introduced easily. It was a fairly entrenched idea, leading to a policy in some zoos against accepting adult chimps. At the same time, it was also a widely-accepted premise that it was safer to introduce a female adult into an established group, because females were considered generally less aggressive. But during her time at Chimfunshi Carole often saw the opposite happening, with females sometimes being the primary aggressors. It's true that Carole considered an ideal group to be one consisting of more females than males. But that had less to do with female lack of aggression than with the fact that males, as they mature, start what can be thought of as some hard politicking to gain rank among the other males. What's more, having more males than females in a group means more competition for sexual partners.

But the world of chimp socialization is always full of surprises. In Florida, as one group was being formed in preparation for their release to the island, there was great concern among the caregivers about a chimp named Hanzie; they worried constantly about him getting into fights, or even just becoming overly excited, because his heart was so bad that it couldn't keep up with the blood supply he required. In such moments his lips and gums would actually turn purple from lack of oxygen. Seeing this, Carole decided to separate him from the rest of the group, and as she put it, ponder his future. In the end she determined that Hanzie "would get his chance at the island and grass under his feet and a big family." To make this happen she all but slept at the chimp house, figuring that if Hanzie got into a fight she could jump up and close doors to stop it before he dropped dead from exertion. In spite of Hanzie's weak heart and low-ranking status, he ended up being quite confident during the introductions. Hanzie would finally know the feeling of belonging in a group.

GLORIA GROW, DIRECTOR OF THE FAUNA FOUNDA-TION, A CHIMPANZEE AND FARM ANIMAL SANCTUARY OUTSIDE MONTREAL, REMEMBERS BEING AT SAVE THE CHIMPS FOR A COUPLE OF DAYS BEFORE THE TRAILER ARRIVED FROM NEW MEXICO WITH THE FIRST AIR FORCE CHIMPS: "Carole was happy and excited. It was beautiful. We'd sit outdoors at night and talk. We cried. It was like she'd just fallen in love."

On the morning of the big day, though, in April of 2001, Carole's contentment was pinched by anxieties, though few would know it. Indeed, the first person she encountered on the morning the chimps were to arrive was Gloria Grow; as the two women passed each other, Carole smiled at Gloria and muttered under her breath, "Dead man walking." Here was her biggest dream finally coming true, and yet on that particular day her usual confidence was in short supply. "How could I be hesitating about anything? But I was full of fears, I was full of insecurities. I was convinced I wasn't up for the job." Then the truck pulled in and they opened the doors. "I took one look at those chimps and every doubt I had vanished. I felt like I'd been with them forever."

Hannah was in a cage in the corner, rocking back and forth furiously, leading Carole to immediately start trying to figure out what she could do to help. Hanzie, meanwhile, was rattling his door and demanding breakfast, but that was pretty much par for the

OPPOSITE *Carole reviewing plans.*
LEFT *Gromek.*

course for Hanzie. Amy showed an instant dislike for Carole, while Gromek clearly enjoyed scaring her by pounding on the side of his cage and making her jump—a game he would relish for years to come. Faith arrived with no hair, her skin pink as a baby mouse. Dana was there, too—the chimp who would arguably be more important to Carole than any other, though at the time she made little impression.

"We started introducing the chimps to each other the very next day. Hannah, my immediate concern, was introduced to Gromek in the hopes that she would gain some confidence. Well she did, and started bossing Gromek around in no time," recounted Carole. Her next priority was Hanzie, forty years old with a heart condition so serious that Carole debated including him in the introductions at all. In the end, though, she decided to try pairing him with Dana, who was about the same age, and also born in Africa. Dana made the first move, and before long she and Hanzie were playing. "After a few

more introductions," noted Carole, "it became clear that Dana was good at this. No, Dana was a genius. When she met great big Waylon, who was too afraid to even look at her, Dana went right up to him, put her hand under his chin and lifted his face so they could look at each other. Waylon melted. So did I."

Carole intentionally didn't read the records Coulston had kept on the chimps, spotty as they were. "I didn't want to be polluted by their contents," she explained. "Liza's record, for example, stated she was raised by humans and therefore could never be part of a social group, which didn't prove to be true at all. Meanwhile, Waylon was described as being 'only 75% there, possibly brain damaged,' which also didn't seem to be the case, at least not at his new home in Florida. Without any of this knowledge about the Air Force chimps we went ahead and introduced them. They're a family. Not a perfect family. But by all standards a pretty normal, dysfunctional average family."

BY DECEMBER 11, THE STAFF AT SAVE THE CHIMPS HAD FINISHED MAKING ALL THE NECESSARY INTRODUC-TIONS—ONE ON ONE, TWO ON ONE, TWO ON TWO, AND EVERY OTHER VARIATION IMAGINABLE—LITERALLY HUNDREDS OF MEETINGS IN ALL. All that was left to do was open the doors, allowing the Air Force chimps to finally gain access to their own island. Even before the doors were opened, the chimps knew something was going on, having tuned in to the buzz created by all the extra activity. Their reactions, when the doors were finally opened, were as varied as the personalities of the chimps themselves. Easy-going Waylon, the gentle giant of the group, had a quick look around outside and then headed back to the building to think things over. Garfield, on the other hand, full of teenage bluster, ran out on the grass with great bravado, making sure everyone noticed, while Marty, who was much older, stayed close to the building, curious but hesitant.

Meanwhile Lil' Mini seemed genuinely surprised when she placed her feet onto soft earth and blades of grass for the first time. At first she retreated, hugging the wall and pacing along a concrete runway near the shelter building, then headed out onto the grass again before scurrying back into the building, where the other chimps were still waiting and wondering. There'd been a great deal for Lil' Mini to absorb as of late, having finally joined a chimp family only several months earlier. And now this heady, unprecedented offering of grass and hills and sky.

By the time several hours passed, all the chimps had left the building and were making at least cautious moves into their new world. Writer David Cassidy, who witnessed the emerging chimps, wondered if perhaps "the feel of the grass, the open air and the clouds folding into themselves overhead awakened dormant instincts"—as if hundreds of thousands of years of hardwired knowledge and memory was being "reactivated by the caress of the wind and the smell of the dirt." True or not, it was a stunning, heart-warming thing to witness.

Then brash young Garfield decided it was time to get on with it, so he crossed the land bridge leading from the chimp's indoor area and headed out to the island. And that was all it took. Gromek and Emily and Hannah, Liza and Phyllis, and then all the rest decided to make their way over to the island as well, where they found no end of treats the staff had hidden for

ABOVE *Gromek, Garfield, Tammy, and Liza.*
OPPOSITE *Lil Mini*

them in the grass. There was climbing to be done on the special wooden tower that had been erected, as well as a fine tunnel to explore. And, of course, there was a lot to talk about. Though they still wore scars, on that day they may have felt a million miles from their former lives as isolated test subjects. Remarkably, right at the point the chimps were out exploring their new island, the moon—that iconic symbol of the space program for more than forty years—drifted across the face of the sun, yielding a breathtaking solar eclipse.

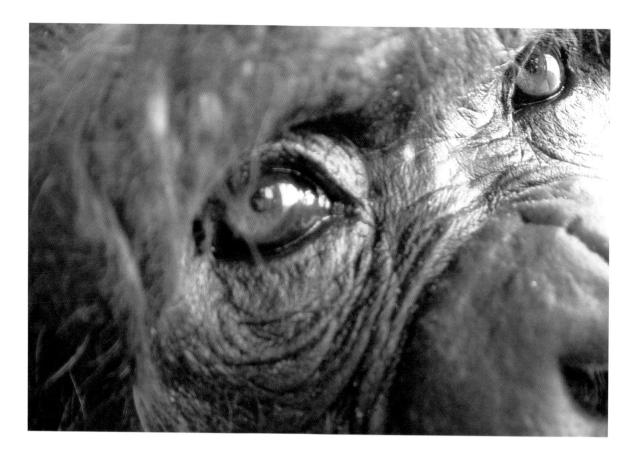

then render a decision and make it stick. (The downside, said Carole, of being the policeman is that "if you can stop a fight just by looking in that direction, you don't really appeal to anyone as a play partner, because you're sort of scary. As you're keeping the peace your girlfriend might be behind the big hill with another guy. So much for the theory that says an alpha male gets to pass on his genes to all the females.")

Like most of the chimps, Waylon had health issues that required medication. And this may have been part of what made him at times a very fussy eater—something the kitchen staff responded to by cooking special rice and pasta meals for him. Every other day someone went to the grocery store to pick up the things he especially fancied, including kiwis, applesauce, juice boxes, romaine lettuce, and ingredients for

blueberry pancakes. Other staff brought in mangos, along with anything else they could think of. Each morning, Jenny, who was managing Waylon's building, would get on the radio to report whether or not Waylon had taken his meds and eaten his breakfast. Based on those reports the staff sometimes needed to get creative, stuffing his meds in juice boxes. But for all their efforts, Waylon's health began a sharp decline. As happens when any chimp is sick, a weight fell over the sanctuary.

One day Waylon's heart just stopped beating. Not a heart attack per se, which might involve clutching your chest in pain and wondering what was going on; his heart simply stopped beating. Save the Chimps veterinarian Dr. Jocelyn Bezner found him shortly after lunch, slumped over.

Despite heroic efforts to revive him with CPR and various drugs, it was no use. And while it wasn't the sanctuary's first death, Carole would later say that when Waylon died, she could feel her chest rip open: "The break was so big. As we tried to revive [him], I kept saying over and over to myself 'NOT THIS ONE, NOT THIS ONE.'" Carole said that in that moment she had no idea who she was talking to, but that she felt she was in combat with someone or something. "Waylon was being stolen, and there was nothing I could do about it."

Waylon's fate was sealed years before the staff at Save the Chimps ever met him, and it was that fact she was resisting: "I finally figured out who I was fighting with as we tried to revive Waylon. It was with the system that took everything from these chimps—their families, their freedom, and in many cases, their health. And what the chimps got in return, including Waylon, was pretty much nothing more than monkey chow and water." Though few knew it, this shadow caused by the suffering and near torture these chimpanzees had endured for decades never left Carole Noon. Veterinarian Dr. Jocelyn Bezner was one of her closest confidants, and also one of the few who saw the dark cloud such knowledge often brought to Carole's heart: "[Carole] said to me over and over again, especially when a chimp would die, 'Bez, I just can't do it anymore. I can't stand in front of this staff and say, "They were in a better place, we saved them." It makes me sick to my stomach.'"

Carole and her staff knew that when one of the chimps passed, it was important to let the other chimps in the family have time to grasp that their friend had died. After Waylon's death, the staff let the other chimps in his group into the adjoining cages so they could see for themselves. So they could say goodbye. Herbie in particular, a former pet chimp, was incredibly upset and kept trying to get Waylon to move by pulling the blanket he was lying on.

Waylon's body was then loaded onto the flatbed of a truck belonging to a caregiver named Cassidy, to be carried to the administration building so the rest of the staff could say their goodbyes when they came to work the following morning. When Cassidy started driving towards the Administration Building, Carole said she did so very slowly, "like she had precious cargo on board." Tera was in the back with Waylon; Mikey followed in his car, as did Jenny and Dr. Bezner in theirs. "I was watching a funeral procession," Carole said "a string of slow-moving cars and crying people. The kind [of procession] they have the police stopping cars for at green lights in town. The kind they have for VIPs. Only this funeral procession was for a chimpanzee named Waylon." Carole said that at that moment she couldn't have been prouder of these humans who loved Waylon, who took his life and death so seriously. "I knew their hearts were breaking too. Nor could I have been prouder of Waylon, who had all these people in love with him.

"The rest of these old and compromised chimpanzees have to outlive me. Dana, Wes, Marty, Gromek, and about 300 other of my favorites. I must insist on that."

CHAPTER 04

Miracle in New Mexico

FTER CAROLE SUCCESSFULLY SUED THE AIR FORCE AND RECEIVED TWENTY-ONE CHIMPS, "JUST ABOUT EVERY HUMANE GROUP IN THE COUNTRY DESCENDED ON ME, WANTING PHOTOS AND HORROR STORIES OF THE CONDITIONS OF THE CHIMPS AFTER THEY ARRIVED FROM THE COULSTON LAB." She refused such requests, choosing instead to play what she liked to call a "short end game." She wrote Fred Coulston regularly to give him details about the arrival of the Air Force chimps, then later kept him informed about the progress they were making. By her own reckoning Coulston was at the time old enough, and perhaps forgetful enough, "to not remember the grounds of my lawsuit—that the Coulston Foundation had the worst record of primate care in the history of the Animal Welfare Act."

The strategy paid off in a way she never could have fathomed. Three months after the release of the twenty-one Air Force chimps onto their island, with Carole happily working to gradually grow the new sanctuary— again, something that was supposed to happen slowly, over many years—she got a phone call from Fred Coulston. With the loss of support by the National Institutes of Health (NIH) (which had already removed half the chimps from his custody), he was facing financial disaster. Things were so bad that in order to raise money he'd sold off babies, leased a pair of

ABOVE *The cage used by the Coulston Foundation to house infected chimpanzees.*

OPPOSITE *Carole cleaning the facilities of the Coulston Foundation.*

chimps to a minor league baseball team for use as mascots, and shipped off still more to work for an infamous animal handler in Hollywood. "A few older chimps went to other biomedical labs," says Jon Stryker, though in truth many had been so used up in decades of AIDS and hepatitis experiments that they were of little interest to researchers, who preferred "clean" test subjects.

Coulston was quick to the point, telling Carole he was willing to sell the facility to her fledgling Save the Chimps organization for twelve million dollars. As for the chimpanzees themselves—266 of them, or roughly 20 percent of the total number being held in American laboratories—they would be included as a donation. Primatologist Roger Fouts later commented that basically Carole bought the cage from the poacher, and he gave her the chimp for free. She wasn't overly fond of the comment, but had to admit it was about right. "Fred reached out to me," Carole wrote later in a letter to a colleague, "and that's part of the story, too. I never burned that bridge. If Fred had never called me, none of this would have happened."

On one hand it was a terribly exciting prospect, though by anyone's reckoning it was impossible to take on that many new residents at her fledgling Florida sanctuary. Nonetheless, in the end she and Jon packed their bags and made the trip to New Mexico—not really intending to buy the lab, but rather hoping to figure out a way to secure the rescue of at least another ten or fifteen chimpanzees. As the two friends began their tour of the lab, dressed head-to-toe in white hazard suits—outfits that by all indications were scaring the heck out of the chimps—the place seemed like a penitentiary, complete with a brawny, scowling man with tattoos who showed up now and then to patrol the lines of cages. It was dark and humid from standing water on the floors, and incredibly noisy. There was a terrible stink, forcing them to breathe through their mouths to avoid gagging. Despite the fact that chimps are normally fastidious groomers, many were covered in their own feces.

At one point during their tour, the staff told Jon and Carole a story about one of the chimps who had a habit of throwing his poop. Then they went on to describe, and with no small amount of pride, how they collected the crap in buckets and threw it back—their version of

BELOW *Carole and her team tour The Coulston Foundation, fully decked out in hazard suits as insisted upon by their hosts.*

LEFT *Coulston before Carole and Jon arrived.*

teaching the chimp a lesson. Meanwhile, over in the nursery, recalls Jon, "they had babies all together with no mother there. We watched them make little trains with five or six of them holding on to each other because they were so afraid. Because they didn't have any sense of security. It's something I'll never forget."

Upon finishing the tour, walking out of a building that from that day on they'd know as "the dungeon," they were badly shaken. Carol turned to Jon with a look of frustration on her face. How in the world do we choose, she wondered out loud, who to save among all those suffering chimps?

Jon didn't hesitate. "We've got to take them all."

Carole later recalled, "We didn't look at each other and say, 'Well, this is going to cost $20 million dollars,' or 'What do you think annual operating costs will be?' Jon just looked at me and said, 'We have to get them all out.' I agreed. And at that moment [I] accepted responsibility for doing just that." She later admitted that "if Jon had said 'I'll pledge $10M to do it, to move them to Florida, I wouldn't have accepted the deal and put my name to a project that wouldn't succeed. We both knew what a huge undertaking this would be—no kidding, the largest rescue of chimpanzees in history. I trusted Jon, and Jon trusted me."

opening doors

NEGOTIATIONS TO BUY THE COULSTON LAB GOT UNDER WAY FAIRLY QUICKLY. The process involved more than six months of negotiations, until finally a deal was struck in which Save the Chimps agreed to simply pay off the lab's roughly $2.5 million in debt. During the talks, and on Carole's invitation, Fred Coulston flew east to Florida to actually see the Air Force chimps who had once resided in his lab. He was shocked to find out that none of them were being put to "good use." No research was going on. No breeding. To him it was incredible, even outrageous. Yet his reaction, which would have raised the hackles of a great many animal advocates,

FRED COULSTON WAS SHOCKED TO SEE THAT NONE OF THE AIR FORCE CHIMPS WERE BEING PUT TO "GOOD USE."

wasn't really an issue for Carole: "Did I ask that part of the negotiations to take over the lab include having the man denounce his livelihood and his belief in biomedical research? That wasn't going to happen, and I didn't even ask. My goal was the 266 chimpanzees and their potential offspring— not Fred coming out against biomedical research and the past crimes he'd committed."

On September 16, 2002, Carole was handed the keys to the lab. And for the chimps living at Coulston, life would never again be as frightening, boring, or full of neglect as it had been in previous decades. Years after the deal was done, Carole confessed in a letter to Jon that she sometimes wondered what the chimpanzees of Coulston must have been doing

OPPOSITE *Carole and Fred Coulston with their respective lawyers at the closing of the deal for what would no longer be the Coulston Foundation. Carole and Jon received the keys that very day.*

LEFT *Carole talks with staff at the Coulston Foundation.*

before Arcus and Save the Chimps arrived. Then she answered her own question: "[They were] simply existing, slowly going out of their minds."

She was acutely aware of just how remarkable this rescue really was, how the heavens and earth seemed to have moved to accommodate the effort. Even the appearance of a new manager in Florida—a woman named Lori Brown—had come at just the right time. Without someone to care for the twenty-one Air Force chimps already at the sanctuary, Carole explained, "I could never have taken Fred Coulston up on the offer, even with the Arcus money. But I had an heir apparent in Florida after only one year. My eye has always been on the big picture. Or, perhaps, slipping as I get out of the bath tub."

AS HAPPY AN OCCASION AS SECURING THE COULSTON FOUNDATION CHIMPANZEES WAS, IT LEFT SAVE THE CHIMPS WITH A STAGGERING CHALLENGE. By Carole's estimation it would take roughly five years to ready the Florida sanctuary for this many new residents; besides which, the old lab would have to be utterly transformed, taking it from a despoiled prison camp to a caring, humane residence. But that would take more than just retrofitting existing buildings. It would also mean hiring good people for the job.

"I spent several hours today just roaming around," Carole wrote shortly after taking over the lab, "talking to chimps, evaluating the lousy cleaning jobs done on the cages, and making final decisions about what staff to keep. The people here for the shortest time,

those with the least experience and exposure to the 'party line' put forth at this place, are the people I want to stay. I suspect half will quit two weeks after we take over, which is fine by me. This place needs new blood, fresh ideas and someone to listen to these ideas. I am all ears."

Among the new caregivers hired was a young couple named Mikey and Tera, who up until then had been working at a bar in Alamogordo. "One day the bar announced they were closing for remodeling," says Mikey, "so basically we were out of a job." Having heard that hiring was going on at Coulston, they headed out for a look. Almost before they knew what was happening they found themselves hired by Carole, completely immersed in the strange world of caring for captive chimpanzees. At the time, Mikey

had a blue goatee and a Mohawk haircut. "I always wondered," he says, "if she thought the way I looked would serve as great entertainment for the chimps."

Shortly after they started work, the couple happened to be in Building 300—the infamous "dungeon"—when Carole came by with a group of people she was interviewing for jobs. In front of everyone she came up to Mikey and Tera, then asked in a loud voice if they knew why she'd hired them. Not waiting for an answer, she explained: "It was because you walked with me during the interview instead of behind me. You were paying attention." And with that, everybody in the interview group shuffled closer.

"Dr. Noon was prone to losing her patience," says Tera. "She wasn't big on second or third chances. You learned fast that when she told you to do something,

THE SEASONED WORKERS
WHO STAYED ON HAD TO
ACCEPT THE FACT THAT
THESE CHIMPS HAD RIGHTS
NOW, THAT THEY DESERVED
RESPECT; THOSE WHO
COULDN'T EMBRACE SUCH
IDEAS DIDN'T LAST LONG.

you did it right. And in all the calls she made about how to handle different situations and crises, she was almost never wrong." Once you learned how to work with her, Tera adds, it was a brilliant experience.

"You just had to know that everything was for the greater cause of the chimps," adds Mikey. "And like she said that day with the tour group, you were expected to work beside her. Her main team, every one of us, was always with her in the trenches. She never expected anybody to do anything that she hadn't done herself. Never." On any given day Dr. Noon would be up at 7:00 AM to clean cages with the rest of the staff, then maybe head off to the kitchen to make meals for lunch, returning again later in the day to help prepare dinners. When everyone else went home in the evening, she'd head off to write reports. "She worked constantly," recalls Tera. "Constantly." Still, Tera says Carole had

an extremely sharp sense of humor and was a consummate practical joker besides.

The seasoned workers who stayed on had to accept the fact that these chimps had rights now, that they deserved respect; those who couldn't embrace such ideas didn't last long. The ones who did, though, soon found themselves part of an extremely tight family—one that spent a lot of time together, even after hours. "There were lots of people at Coulston who couldn't understand Dr. Noon," recalls Mikey. "They weren't used to the kind of care we were giving to the chimps. But chimps aren't for everybody. They're

OPPOSITE *Carole on laundry duty. She really took on every job at the sanctuary.*

LEFT *Carole hosing down the interior hallways of Save the Chimps. There was a certain way to do it—the Carole Way—and she would get frustrated with employees who didn't get it right.*

ABOVE *Flowers memorialize the suffering of chimpanzees neglected to death in Alamogordo.*

Chimps are incredibly good at picking up on people's moods, able to figure out in short order if you're not on your game. "If you're having a bad day," Tera says, "they pick up on that and pretty soon the whole building is having a bad day." She recalls the occasional person coming into work after having tied one on the night before, struggling with a hangover. "Without fail, on that day the chimps would make a point of being a little extra noisy."

Mikey started his work in Building 700E, which was notorious for housing the rowdiest chimps—the angry ones, the poop throwers. "When I first started in that building," he recalls, "we'd wear these big Tyvek suits, dressed like we were going to the moon or something. We'd walk down the aisle and poop would be coming at us from all sides." But such behavior may have been as much about the neglect the chimps had suffered for so long at Coulston, as it was about the white suits the newcomers were wearing. The people who had been running the building before Carole's arrival had, by all indications, been left to their own devices, and over time that translated into having very little interaction with the chimps. "The way I was first trained," says Mikey, "by one of the old employees, was to make a fast trip down the aisle with a clipboard and look at the butts of the females [to see if they were in estrus], then toss them some monkey chow. That was it."

The new staff, on the other hand, along with a few old-timers who were willing and able to change their perspectives, stopped and talked to the chimps at every opportunity, gaining in short time the ability to address every single one of them by name. From day one the lights never went out at night without the humans on

intimidating. They have enormous mood swings." He says even people who love chimps wouldn't be able to just walk into a family group and start working with them. "They'd rally with each other against you until you broke. They could make you cry. It takes a certain kind of person to realize that you've walked into their world. That this isn't about you, not about the human things you might want to impose on them. They have their own way, and your job is to fit into that."

hand offering soothing words. On holidays—"Chimp-o-ween," Thanksgiving, Christmas, Easter, the Fourth of July—parties were held, usually with wrapped presents and streamers and other decorations. On those days, as well during annual "bananaversary" parties, the chimps were nearly beside themselves with excitement.

In the summer of 2004, Jen Feuerstein announced an intriguing scientific breakthrough in New Mexico. "We've discovered the evolutionary roots of break-dancing," she said—"the 80s dance craze in which street performers would do unusual dance moves on a large piece of cardboard." At that time food was being delivered to the chimps wrapped in large flat pieces of cardboard, and one day the caregivers gave several sheets to a group of 5 year-olds, "Stephanie immediately jumped on the cardboard, lay down on her back, and spun herself around as fast as she could, which was a popular break-dancing move. The other kids saw what she was doing and picked up the skill right away." Jen went on to say that while none was reported to have mastered the Worm or the Robot, they nonetheless went on sliding and spinning with amazing enthusiasm.

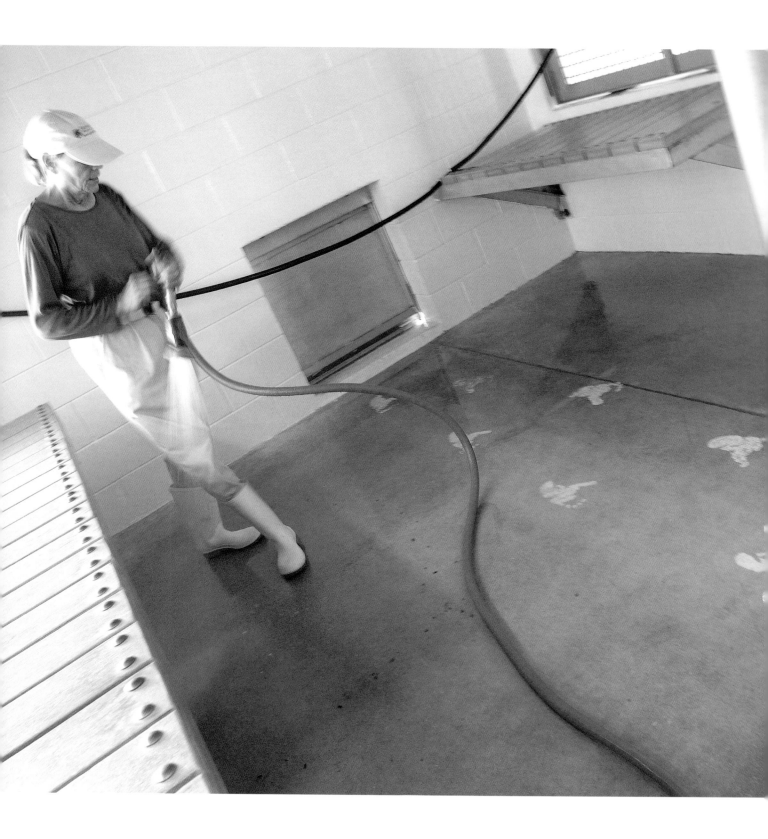

OPPOSITE *Carole, cleaning. She was particular about who used the hose, and had a certain way she wanted it done.*

LEFT AND BELOW *Staff and volunteers spend hours preparing food that doubles as enrichment. Here, peanut butter, cereal, raisins, and jelly are smeared into astroturf. They love getting every last bit of food out of the green stuff and will spend a fair part of the day doing it.*

MEANWHILE, AN ASTOUNDING NUMBER OF CHANGES WERE HAPPENING TO THE LAB ITSELF, STARTING WITH AN INTENSE AMOUNT OF CLEANING AND SCRUBBING. A security fence was installed around the perimeter of the property, and skylights punched into the ceilings. The main laboratory room, which for decades had been filled with the odor of blood and antiseptics, was transformed into a kitchen, offering up instead smells from giant pots of oatmeal spiced with cinnamon, tomato sauces, and vegetable stews cooking on the stoves. There were fruit smoothies in the blender, and peanut butter sandwiches laid out on the counters. This would also be where so-called "foraging boards" were made, created by smearing peanut butter and banana onto pieces of artificial turf and hanging them on the outside of the cages, allowing the chimps the delightful work of retrieving goodies through the mesh of the cage. Likewise, dozens of raisin boards created—[pieces of recycled plastic brick with holes drilled into them and stuffed with raisins], the retrieval of which required the kind of poking and prodding a chimp in the wild

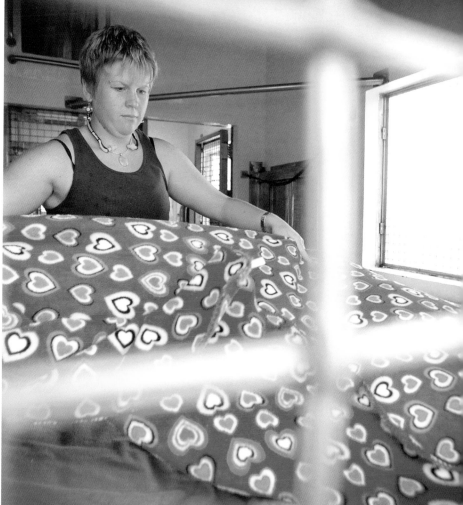

WHEN DONATIONS OF
TOYS STARTED POURING
IN, IT WAS OFTEN THE
CHIMPS THEMSELVES
WHO GUIDED
THE DISTRIBUTION.

would routinely engage in at an ant nest or termite mound. Hammocks were installed inside the cages, providing the vast majority of the chimps with the first soft surfaces they'd ever known.

What used to be nothing but bare cages—tiny, brittle worlds of concrete and steel—were suddenly filled with toys and blankets and magazines and boxes. When donations of toys started pouring in, it was often the chimps themselves who guided the distribution. "We all agree the toy drum goes to Pumpkin," said Carole, "the stuffed toy lamb goes to Tami, while the great big dog is for Rebel. The pink hat, of course, goes to Tina. Her current pink hat, her

OPPOSITE LEFT *Dana relaxing in her yellow hammock.*

OPPOSITE RIGHT *Shaking out a line-dried blanket.*

LEFT TOP *Blankets being brought in.*

LEFT BOTTOM *Donated toys.*

prized possession, is shrinking with every washing, which has us all worried. And the little purse with the Velcro strap is for Tash."

Duane Harris—long-time maintenance supervisor for Coulston, who would stay on until the last chimps were wheeled off to Florida—was working overtime to get openings cut in the concrete walls that for decades had separated the chimps from each other. Gates with mesh screens were then inserted into the openings, allowing the chimps to sit next to one another, shoulder to shoulder, often with their fingers touching through the holes. In time they would gain the chance to actually slip through the openings

and meet their neighbors, which they often did by hugging one another, giving the kinds of embraces reserved for the truly thankful and the utterly forlorn.

Once that work was finished, Duane set about raising the height of the outdoor cages to offer the chimps more room, more views of the world outside. He figured a way to enclose them with adjustable canvas covers with clear plastic windows that, when heaters were added, afforded the chimps a wider sense of space even in the cold, windy days of winter. (Staff at the old Coulston lab hadn't allowed the chimps to go outside if it was below 55 degrees, or if it was above 80, which pretty much stripped them of any outdoor time both summer and winter.) "It means the chimps have somewhere new to go," Carole explained. "They can see out the sides of their cages, they can be in direct contact with their neighbors on both sides, they have a new view, they can climb. Those on the dark side can finally catch some sun and they can see all the chimps who live on either side of them."

"When I worked for Coulston," says Duane, "I was just a maintenance man. Something broke and I went in and fixed it and then got my butt out of there. When Dr. Noon came along, from then on it was all about the chimps. And I was part of the team."

Room at the Inn
PET CHIMPANZES

Over the years, Save the Chimps has also taken in a handful of pets who needed sanctuary, even though pet chimps can be far more challenging than those coming out of biomedical labs. In the middle of her negotiations to buy the Coulston Foundation lab, Carole was working with a couple with two pet chimpanzees named Herbie and Sonny, who she'd earlier agreed to make a home for. "I wanted to move Herbie and Sonny to Florida before we took over the lab," she said, "just to make sure they had a 'room at the inn' before our little sanctuary went through a major expansion."

The couple had acquired Herbie long before, when he was just three months old. To make him easier to handle they elected to have his testicles removed when he was young, and because of that he lacked the testosterone levels necessary to develop what are referred to as secondary sexual characteristics. Instead of the normal broad shoulders and big thighs typical of a male chimp, Herbie grew up tall and lanky, with pencil-thin legs. Sonny, on the other hand, was a late-arriving stepchild, rescued by the couple when he was eighteen

years old, as he lay dying in a Florida roadside zoo. Herbie wasn't happy when the interloper showed up, beginning a two-week hunger strike on the day Sonny appeared.

By any definition, these were pampered pets, treated by the couple as if they were their own children. Both guardians were serious about the responsibility they'd taken on, going so far as to establish opposite work schedules so one would always be home with "the boys." They had full contact with the chimps every day, eating dinner with them, even tucking them into bed at night. But while such care was offered with the kindest of intentions, it wasn't without danger. Pound for pound, chimpanzees are about four times stronger than a comparable-sized human; what's more, some researchers

OPPOSITE AND LEFT *Herbie.*

have suggested chimps may have less strength control than we do, which can sometimes lead to sudden, violent bursts of physicality.

On arriving at Save the Chimps in mid-2002, Carole recalls, "Sonny took one look at me and fell in love. There's no explaining chemistry, and I felt the same way about him." Herbie, on the other hand, had a rather different take. Suddenly he was living in a cage next to other chimpanzees, being asked to eat apples and bananas and sweet potatoes instead of the chilidogs and burritos with sour cream he liked so much. "Somebody was changing Herbie's life," said Carole. "And Herbie figured out that somebody was Carole Noon."

In an attempt to ease the transition, the couple stayed at the sanctuary for a few weeks after the boys moved in. When they left, Herbie went downhill fast—refusing to eat, not talking to anyone, barely coming out of his hammock even for a drink of water. "Pretty soon I was hustling up chilidogs and burritos," said Carole, "which Herbie finally accepted." Sonny, meanwhile, was loving all of it. Loving the apples and the oatmeal in the morning, eager to meet the chimps living next door. In some ways he seemed to have an attitude similar to many biomedical lab chimps; after years of hard times at that roadside zoo, the sanctuary just didn't seem all that bad.

Meanwhile, just as Herbie was getting on board with his new surroundings, his human dad came for a visit, triggering

"THESE FORMER PET CHIMPS," CAROLE ONCE WROTE, "THEY TAX YOU, THEY DRAIN YOU AND CAUSE YOU NO END OF WORRY. AND THEN THEY GET ON WITH THEIR LIVES . . . EVEN AFTER 24 YEARS."

yet another two weeks of withdrawal and depression, including another hunger strike. Seeing this, Carole explained to the man as gently as possible that he'd have to stay away until Herbie was socialized into a group, living successfully on one of the islands. And happily, that day did finally come. Both Herbie and Sonny joined two babies and their adopted mom [Henrietta], as well as Arthur, Phoenix, Dana, and Waylon. On being released from the shelter house Herbie and Sonny and the kids ran out through the door like the wind, Herbie's lanky body moving like a spider across the island, everyone stopping now and then to reassure each other with a group hug. Herbie and Sonny's former human caretakers watched from a blind so they wouldn't be seen.

Months later the couple returned again to the sanctuary for a visit. Sonny was glad to see his human friends, but then that didn't surprise anyone. As for Herbie, Carole was fairly sure he'd gotten on with his life, so she was willing to risk a reunion with his former family, figuring it wasn't likely to lead to another hunger strike or bout of depression. "Herbie gave [the man] a huge greeting," said Carole. "'Oh, so nice to see you my old friend, it's been way too long'"—lots of pants and smiles. Then Herbie thanked him for visiting and before he left, explained that he had family matters to attend to. And then that little butt held up by those skinny legs turned and walked away." That night, much to everyone's relief, Herbie ate his dinner.

Currently, there are a number of sanctuaries, including the Center for Great Apes in Wauchula, Florida, as well as organizations like Project ChimpCARE, trying hard to help anxious pet owners find safe haven for their chimps. "These former pet chimps," Carole once wrote, "they tax you, they drain you and cause you no end of worry. And then they get on with their lives . . . even after 24 years."

ABOVE AND RIGHT *Clay.*

opening doors

The building known as the dungeon housed fifty-five chimps, and it was nothing short of miraculous to watch as each one finally laid eyes on others who'd been their neighbors for years, but were never seen. Some chimps were thrilled, greeting each other with pant hoots and friendly gestures. For others it was all a big surprise. "Now that Ron's neighbors could see how enormous he is," wrote Carole, "they're sort of apologizing for all the nasty things they said to him over the years. And beautiful Tanya, born in Africa, suddenly has all the boys next door fighting over her."

The first to explore the new outdoor spaces was a massive teenage chimp named Clay. When the crew opened the door between the indoor and outdoor enclosures, Clay sat in the doorway looking up, his eyes as big as saucers. The staff, invited in to watch the big event, were all encouraging him, which to the surprise of some seemed to actually help rather than scare him. Though at first Clay didn't even consider climbing up the new heights to see what the view was, he made huge displays of jumping up and down and then running back inside. Freed from the constraints of a cage, he allowed himself for the first time in his life to jump as high as he could.

By the end of the day, though, Clay's curiosity got the better of him, and he finally made it up to the top of the cage, where he was thrilled at the chance to hang from the new ceiling. For the first time in his adult life he could fully extend his arms and legs and really swing. "It looked like he couldn't get over this new freedom," said Carole, describing him as looking like "a wind chime blowing about

ABOVE *Boy*.

in the wind." When Clay finally made it to the top, the staff stood nearby and all applauded, which pleased Clay to no end.

Next out of the chute was Clay's neighbor, a chimp born in Africa named Boy, who'd spent most of his life at the (now defunct) Laboratory for Experimental Medicine and Surgery in Primates (LEMSIP) in Tuxedo, New York, living in a five-by-seven-foot cage suspended two feet off the ground. "When I met Boy," Carole said, "he was a blob. He sat on his ledge, huddled up all bald and old and only came down for meals. He never went outside, showed no interest in the toys or blankets we gave him. Never said a word. If I had favorites, which of course I don't, Boy would be

CAROLE CONSIDERED ONE OF HER BIGGEST ACHIEVEMENTS IN NEW MEXICO THE DAY BOY ACTUALLY PLAYED WITH HER.

one." (Carole did confess to being particularly fond of certain chimps, though the list was a fluid one. "The truth is I do have favorites. All those people I found in the [Coulston] dungeon like Boy, Carlos, Mack, Casey, Tami, Tarzan, Rufus and Bobby and about 50 others." On still another occasion she wrote: "It will come as no surprise to anyone that my favorite chimps are the chimps which were the result of the Air Force

lawsuit. I have known them the longest, marveled at their transformation into a family and watched them evolve. In fact, some of us are growing old together.")

Carole considered one of her biggest achievements in New Mexico the day Boy actually played with her, when she heard him laughing for the first time. Unlike Clay, Boy didn't hesitate for a minute when it came time to explore the new outdoor enclosure. In fact, he took a fast look through the window at Clay, then proceeded to climb to the very top, where he spent the rest of the day. When dinnertime came, he rushed inside to grab his dinner and carried it to the top of the outdoor cage, where he ate while gazing and panting softly at a comely female named Brandy sitting two cages away. Apparently the attraction was mutual. Brandy didn't even bother to go in to get her dinner, choosing instead to stay at the top of the cage and stare at Boy. On seeing this, Carole's thoughts

OPPOSITE LEFT *Boy.*

OPPOSITE RIGHT *Jaybee enjoying his blankets.*

LEFT *Elway playing with a large paper bag.*

turned to her favorite musician: "As Bob Dylan would say, 'You don't have to be a genius to see that they're madly in love.'" Pretty soon Boy started talking. And every now and then he'd gather up used empty monkey chow bags and busy himself making a nest.

As the outdoor extensions were first being installed, many of the staff were making excited comments about the change, using words like "awesome" and "amazing." Though Carole smiled and nodded, in her diary she wrote: "It's a stinking additional four feet. Pathetic is more like it." Still, when those doors were opened and the chimps finally walked through, she admitted to being as moved as she was when she watched the Air Force chimps making their way to their three-acre island. "It means everything to them."

As time went on, the chimps started coming into their own in other ways too—becoming more curious, showing their personalities. At the end of that day when she finally got the keys to the lab, after everyone else had left, she entered Building 700. There, in the first cell, she spotted JayBee, desperately trying to build a nest out of leftover monkey chow and trash. She hurried off to find a blanket for him, which he immediately employed, in the process becoming the first adult chimp at Coulston to enjoy that little kindness. (Not everyone was so easily comforted. As Carole continued down the chimp hall to greet the chimps she "got slammed big time," with Ryan throwing his poop at her so hard it knocked out her contact lens.")

From then on, JayBee would be king of the blankets, often receiving extras so he could make what he considered an adequate bed for a good nap. A couple years later, on a particularly cold and rainy day, instead of using all of his blankets for a nest, he ripped a hole in the center of one and slipped it over his head for a poncho. "He looked so warm and cozy," Carole said, "that we didn't have the heart to tell him that the retro '70s look was going out of style." Blankets are a substitute for the tree branches chimps in the wild use to make nests each night. Some captive chimps take this task very seriously. Garfield incorporated toys in his nest, while Emily added paper bags and cornhusks to hers. In Florida, however, Elway would prove the master nest builder. First he spread a blanket at the base, then built "walls" around the perimeter using dried cattails; after that he cruised the island looking for other cool stuff to add to the pad, often using an empty cardboard box to collect toys, pine cones, and pretty much anything else he could find.

When it came to the critical work of making introductions among the chimps—the first step in establishing social groups—Carole decided to deal with the most extreme cases first. And of those, Bobby—the chimp we met earlier, a victim of countless biomedical experiments who'd fallen into fits of biting

BLANKETS ARE A SUBSTITUTE FOR THE TREE BRANCHES CHIMPS IN THE WILD USE TO MAKE NESTS EACH NIGHT.

RIGHT, TOP *Mack and Jordan.*
RIGHT, BOTTOM LEFT *Kay grooming Rowan.*
RIGHT, BOTTOM RIGHT *Lisa and Bambi.*

himself—was at the top of the list. Bobby never went outside, even when the cages were expanded. He was often afraid. He slept sitting up. The staff moved him up to the larger cages in a nearby building and introduced him to Ragan—a small, eight-year-old male who was being bullied by the older males he was living with. It was a perfect choice. On first meeting, the two chimps walked up to each other and embraced in a long hug.

Next into the mix came Lisa and her three-year-old daughter, Bambi. Like Ragan, Lisa was being bullied at the time; unfortunately, on seeing Bobby she seemed to conclude that here at last was someone she could bully back. There was just one problem with her plan. Her little daughter Bambi fell in love with Bobby immediately, refusing to leave his side, and more often than not, their relationship made Lisa behave. Bobby would continue, on occasion, to have bouts of depression and self-biting, but it grew to be less of an issue than it had been. Following one such incident in 2008, Carole wrote a note to her staff: "I know Bobby is still breaking hearts, but I want you to remember how I found him: alone, in the dungeon, in the dark before the skylights and night lights were installed. He used to sleep sitting up with his nose about an inch from the wall. It may be impossible to ever undo the damage done to him. But he's lucky to

"I THINK THE CHIMPS WERE JUST ANNOUNCING THEMSELVES TO THE WORLD— SAYING WE ARE HERE."

have so many people trying so hard to do just that."

Despite the stew pot of problems they faced on an almost daily basis, it's impossible to overstate a feeling among the staff that something miraculous was happening. On the first day of the chimps having access to their new outdoor spaces, it was decided to leave the doors open all night—a far cry from the old rule of shutting off the outside every day at 4:00 PM. The chimps didn't know what to make of it, and most of them stayed up all night hooting and hollering and pounding on the doors. They were "commenting on the sunset," said Carole. "They had lots to say about the moon and stars appearing in the night sky. From what I could hear there was much disagreement about which exactly were the stars and which was the moon. But for the most part, with the doors finally opened, I think the chimps were just announcing themselves to the world—saying we are here. We exist and have existed behind these closed doors for more years than you care to know. I swear—it was a song they were singing that night."

WITH THE AIR FORCE CHIMPS IN FLORIDA FINALLY OUT ON THEIR ISLAND, THE NUMBER ONE CHIMP DOG—A CANINE NAMED ESTHER, WHO HELPED MOVE EVERYONE DURING CAGE CLEANING—SUDDENLY FOUND HERSELF UNDEREMPLOYED. Carole decided to take her to New Mexico to help out there. Given that the Coulston chimps had never seen a dog before, upon first spotting her, a chaos of hollering and spitting and banging on the cages erupted. That hardly deterred Esther though, who was more than happy to eat all the pieces of monkey chow the chimps kept throwing at her to drive her away. In time they got used to her; some actually enjoyed her visits, while others kept trying to grab her through the mesh of the cage. Before long Esther had assumed much the same job she'd had in Florida, helping move chimps back and forth from the indoor enclosures when it was time to clean.

"This dark, depressing smelly place has been transformed," Carole wrote, cheering herself at the one-year anniversary of having acquired the Coulston Foundation lab. "The doors are open and the light and fresh air is getting in. The staff arrives early, stays late and is always thinking up new things to keep

OPPOSITE *Arthur.*

ABOVE *Esther and Thelma running behind a golf cart carrying Carole and Buddy. Cassidy is driving.*

TARZAN

"ALL WE HAD TO DO WAS OPEN HIS DOOR. HE STEPPED THROUGH AND BECAME A DIPLOMAT, A LEADER, A FATHER TO FOUR BABIES, AND TAMI'S BEST FRIEND."

TARZAN WAS AMONG THE FIRST CHIMPANZEES CAROLE AND JON STRYKER MET ON THEIR INITIAL TOUR OF THE COULSTON FOUNDATION LAB. He was living in the dungeon, next to two frail old females named Tami and Henrietta. Tarzan's job at Coulston had been to breed chimps, which he was good at, producing some fifteen offspring in the course of his decades behind walls of concrete and steel. But like a lot of other lab chimps, he had a long history of heart problems, severe enough that the staff decided when it came time to make the journey to Florida that if he didn't voluntarily enter the transport cage they wouldn't put him through the stress of anesthesia. He would stay put in New Mexico until he told them otherwise. As it turned out, that wasn't a problem. Tarzan jumped through the open door into the cage, as did Tami and Henrietta, and the three senior citizens left for Florida together.

With the Air Force chimps already living as a group on the island, when Tami, Henrietta, and Tarzan arrived there were nine other chimps in the introduction building. It was a ragged group that included five former pet chimps, which to Carole made it the hardest group she'd ever worked with. Former pets had attitudes, spending much of their time chastising the humans for not getting things right. September would only drink from the hose. Pepsi wouldn't eat vegetables, and if someone offered him a carrot they knew he wouldn't eat, he ended up with hurt feelings. Herbie, meanwhile, was holding a grudge against Carole for removing chilidogs from his diet. "Melodrama is their middle name," said Carole. "Add four babies around four years old to the mix and there is always screaming, complaining and yelling coming from the building. And constant bickering over the smallest offenses. I'm thinking that suing the Air Force was easier than getting this group together."

Once, in a conversation with friend Patti Ragan, director of the outstanding Center for Great Apes sanctuary in Wauchula, Florida—home to many former pet and entertainment chimps as well as orangutans— Patti admitted to Carole that she couldn't imagine

taking nearly three hundred chimps from Coulston. "Patti," Carole told her, "to me that's a piece of cake. I can't imagine ever taking care of Knuckles," referring to a chimp with cerebral palsy Patti was caring for.

"She only had a few ex-pet and ex-entertainment chimps," explains Patti. "She said that they took more time and more concern and more management than all the other lab chimps together. They're so different, they're so affected by being raised as little pseudo-humans. We realized then and there that we each have our niche."

When the three senior citizens showed up on the scene, Tarzan immediately took control. "I've worked with plenty of captive groups," said Carole, "and rarely does a clear-cut obvious leader emerge, and certainly not that fast. In some, females were running the group.

In others I couldn't tell who was in charge, which makes sense, as dominance is a dynamic thing that changes from situation to situation. And in some groups, like the one in the Introduction building, nobody is in control and the group runs amuck." Carole had only seen three groups where the alpha male was obvious, and Tarzan was one of them. Besides being a good leader he was kind, using just the right amount of force for what the situation called for, never bullying anyone. Much like Waylon, he could stop a fight just by looking in the direction of the commotion. With Tarzan on the scene the staff could finally take a breath. They no longer had to separate everyone at feeding time, for example; suddenly Sonny and little Kiley were willing to agree that their share of the meals was a fair share after all.

As for Tarzan himself, he stopped pulling out his hair—something chimps who are lonely and bored commonly do—and became a handsome hairy guy again. Carole marveled at everything he did, including how he played with everyone, especially the babies, keeping them under control when they tried to gang up on the former pet chimp Herbie. In short, he ran that group like he was born for the job.

"This is the same chimp," Carole pointed out, " who spent 40 years locked in a cement box being a sperm donor. And all that time he had this inside of him. All we had to do was open his door. He stepped through and became a diplomat, a leader, a father to four babies, and Tami's best friend." One day while Tarzan was playing with the babies, his heart just stopped. He died instantly.

Though it was of course a sad day for the staff, they tried to comfort themselves with the thought that at least he had a family; at least his last moments were spent laughing. What a greater tragedy it would have been had he died all alone in the dungeon.

With Tarzan gone, almost overnight the chaos, the petty fights, and the bickering returned. So Carole brought in what she called "some New Mexico muscle" to sort the group out, in the form of a chimp named Casey. And Casey did love the babies. He adored Tami and got along with the group. But he showed no interest in sorting them out. "On his way to the tunnel one day for a nap," said Carole, "Casey explained that he was in Florida to retire and that I may want to look up what that word means." He wished her luck, she said, then promptly nodded off to sleep.

CHAPTER 05

Beyond Chimp City

WHILE CAROLE WAS IN NEW MEXICO, LORI BROWN WAS TWO THOUSAND MILES TO THE EAST, DOING MUCH OF THE SAME WORK IN FLORIDA. Happily, on most days, there too the stress of making introductions and tending to health issues and raising money, all amidst the chaos of major construction, were softened by the antics of the chimps themselves. One morning the caregivers were astonished to find a female chimp named September gently cuddling a baby possum. She cradled it on her shoulder, even tried to feed the baby part of her breakfast. When the little possum later disappeared, everyone feared the worst. But it was later found in Dana's nest, where she was showing it all the kindness she could muster. Given that the little possum wasn't interested in the chimps' efforts to feed her, eventually the staff took her to a local wildlife rescue center, where she was cared for until old enough to be set free. Not that all Florida wildlife was welcomed at the sanctuary. Once, during breakfast, a caregiver named Chance found Tammy the chimp terribly upset, screaming and crying. When he asked her what was wrong she pointed toward the corner of the building; Chance went over to investigate and discovered a rat snake, which much to Tammy's relief, he quickly captured and took outside. Still another time, a mouse happened to

ABOVE *Lil' Mini, Worthy, and JB.*

OPPOSITE *Garfield with baby Angie.*

OPPOSITE *One of the devoted caregivers visits with the chimps in Lou's family.*

ABOVE LEFT *Marty and Jude.*

ABOVE RIGHT *Hannah, Garfield, and Little Rock.*

scurry by poor Lil' Mini, leaving her so startled that she let out a mighty scream and jumped into Hannah's arms.

Meanwhile, Garfield was busy with the babies in his group, inventing games, one of which the staff came to call the Magic Carpet Ride. On any given day he'd carry a large blanket or sheet out to the island, then encourage little Angie, Jude, or JB—and sometimes all three—to climb aboard. Then he'd grab a corner of the blanket with one of his feet and begin pulling the babies all around the island. If one of them fell off, though, the ride didn't stop. Instead, the little ones would have to run to catch up and jump back on, which they did with a great sense of urgency. While the staff in Florida was never at a standstill, when Garfield was pulling his magic carpet, no one could resist stopping what he or she was doing to watch the fun.

So too did work come to a stop when Lil' Mini taught the toddlers her favorite pastime, which the staff came to know as the Ghost Game. The basic idea was to put a blanket over your head so you can't see, then walk around bumping into things. Little Jude was especially fond of the game whenever there was a chance of bumping into Gromek, who wrapped his arms around the little ghost and gave him a hug until both of them were laughing.

OPPOSITE *Gabe and Gabriella.*
RIGHT *Garfield and babies.*
BOTTOM *Angie with her blanket.*

HAPPILY, WE'VE COME A LONG WAY FROM HOW PEOPLE ONCE THOUGHT OF CHIMPANZEES, WEAVING IMAGES OF THEM FROM EARLY EXPLORERS' FANCIFUL TALES OF HAIRY MONSTERS. Beyond that, though, thanks to the work of some dedicated scientists and primatologists over the past fifty years, we can no longer even think of them as mere imitators, master mimickers of human behavior. We know without a doubt that they possess their own brilliant brand of intelligence, creativity, playfulness, and heart. Yet even with all of this wider, more holistic understanding, we stand at the brink of losing them.

The fate of chimps in their native homelands remains uncertain at best, with only about 150,000 to 250,000 chimps remaining in the wild. The largest populations are in Central Africa, mostly Cameroon, Gabon, and the Democratic Republic of Congo. Elsewhere—from Angola to Guinea, Ghana to Nigeria, Rwanda to Nigeria to Ivory Coast—the chimp population is shrinking right before our eyes. Chimps in Ivory Coast have declined by roughly 90 percent in just twenty-five years; in Togo, Gambia, and several other countries they've disappeared altogether. As Carole Noon, Jane Goodall, Geza Teleki, and many others have warned over and over again, we have

little time left before wild chimpanzees are gone from the face of the earth.

There are various reasons for such staggering declines, beginning with the ongoing practice of hunting chimps for bushmeat. Like gorillas and bonobos, which are also routinely hunted by humans for food, chimps are extremely sensitive to this sort of deadly bluster. Besides being victims of the bullets themselves, in their desperate attempts to escape danger chimps may push into places occupied by other chimp clans, which can lead to deadly territorial battles. While bushmeat has long been part of subsistence living in West and Central Africa, in more

recent decades it's become commercialized, the meat ending up either in mining or logging work camps, or, just as often, on the plates of urban residents willing to pay a steep price for a taste of the exotic. One recent study in Congo suggested that the annual take of chimps now amounts to between 5 and 7 percent of the population; considering their slow reproductive rates, at this pace they won't be able to produce enough offspring to offset the losses.

At the same time, a burst of development has come to tropical Africa from logging and mining, as well as from the widespread clearing of land for planting crops and grazing cattle. In many places

The Trouble with Babies

One of the many big decisions Carole made early on was to have vasectomies performed on all the adult male chimps—an important step, she believed, before starting the all-important introductions that would eventually lead to family groups. But while vasectomies made perfect sense in the bigger picture, she admitted to grieving over the decision. On dozens of occasions she'd witnessed firsthand the joy and wonder that the birth of a baby chimp brought to the entire group. Curiosity tends to blossom in chimpanzees in the wake of such events, with many of the adults going through all sorts of gymnastics just to get a look—even to steal a quick touch, assuming they can do so without upsetting Mom. Little pink fingers can routinely reach into an adult male's mouth to steal food, and there are no questions asked.

"But think about the birth of chimps in captivity," she wrote, "facing fifty or so years behind bars. This is a life sentence. There's no retuning them to the wild—just us doing our very best to keep them happy in their cages, however large those cages, or islands, might be." On occasion she imagined what it would be like for the chimps from New Mexico or Florida to suddenly arrive in the African bush—how they'd be waiting around looking for their three meals a day to be delivered as usual. She envisioned them going out to forage for food, looking for the tree that holds bananas, apples, and pears all at the same time. Or, maybe searching for the oatmeal tree, or the rice with vegetables tree, or the pasta tree. She also imagined Thoto, Pepsi, and September looking around for the plastic spoon tree, which would be needed so they could then eat from the oatmeal and pasta trees.

In the end, though, things didn't go exactly as planned. Some of the vasectomies performed on the chimps by consulting veterinarians didn't hold, leaving Save the

Chimps' veterinarian Dr. Bezner with the task of redoing all of them with the proper technique. One day while Carole was in New Mexico, she got a call from her Florida staff with the rather stunning news that Gogi was pregnant. Carole was shocked, of course, though before long she warmed to the idea. Luckily Gogi was one of the senior females of the group, having spent at least two years with her own mother before being captured in Africa. From the moment her baby arrived—a little one the staff named Jude—Gogi knew exactly what to do.

Then news came that another chimp, Jennifer, was also pregnant. Unlike Gogi, though, Jennifer had been born in a cage, taken away from her mother within hours of her birth. She was later placed in the Coulston Foundation breeding program, and over her thirty-four years there she would give birth to twelve babies. This one, her thirteenth, would be the only one not immediately taken from her, tattooed with a lab number, and given to humans to raise. Jennifer caused Carole no end of worry. Given her past, it wasn't at all certain if she'd even recognize the little bundle as hers. In the end, though, thanks to lots of help from the devoted staff in Florida, Jennifer ended up figuring it out and turned into a good mom after all.

And even that wasn't the end of it. In what Carole called "the saga of the failed vasectomies" Hannah gave birth to her first baby, a little girl named Angie. This birth also caused the staff considerable worry, given that Hannah was

a nervous chimp with a low social ranking. But she made all the right moves—holding little Angie just as mother chimps are supposed to, cuddling her at every chance.

Unfortunately, Hannah had no milk to offer her newborn, so the staff stepped in and took care of the baby until she was mobile enough to go back to her mom. Each day Angie was strapped to the chest of one of the caregivers and taken up to the cages during cleaning and again at meal times—both to make sure her mother didn't forget her, but also to allow her to get used to her chimp family. Against this backdrop of special treatment, Angie became somewhat of a little princess, growing in no time to think she was above all others. When an adult chimp reached out a caring finger to touch her, as often as not she slapped it away. Eventually, she settled in and took up residence with her mother, though it was a slow and careful affair.

Meanwhile, the big teenage boy Garfield became so smitten with Angie that soon after meeting her he made a sleeping nest right next to hers. Daisy, Tammy, Emily and Lil' Mini became the equivalent of good aunts; one day, Lil' Mini picked Angie up and carried her to the big platform out on the island. Notably, reaching this state of peaceful integration, which had never even been attempted before, took about sixteen months. "No other group of people ever worked so hard for so long to accomplish the single goal of returning a baby to her family," wrote Carole. "And I promise, brave little Angie, princess that she is, could not have tried harder either."

Even with all that, Carole thought such fascination missed the bigger point. "Three new babies have been born to a three-acre island, which will be their home for the rest of their lives. By the time they're five years old they'll know every blade of grass." If Save the Chimps was providing its adult residents with a dignified retirement, it was a lot harder to know what to call this thing they were giving to the babies.

chimpanzee habitat has been fractured into a disconnected patchwork, causing them problems not only when it comes to getting enough food, but severely limiting the chance for genetic mixing. Once remote, hard-to-access lands have been turned into places easy to reach, which in turn brings in fresh waves of bushmeat hunters and poachers for the pet trade. At the current rate of development, by 2030 only 10 percent of the world's chimpanzee habitat will still be intact. Jon Stryker's Arcus Foundation is one of a handful of key groups working hard to stop the destruction of key ape habitats in Africa and Asia. In addition to securing lands, Arcus also recently collaborated with international partners to launch the "Great Apes Mapper," which provides real-time monitoring of critical ape populations.

The rapid disappearance of wild chimps is happening in the face of national and international laws meant to protect them, including the Endangered Species Act (ESA) and the Convention on International Trade in Endangered Species of Wild Fauna and Flora (CITES). The Endangered Species Act currently allows exceptions for researchers, dealers, and exhibitors, and doesn't apply at all to chimps bred in the United States, though declaring all chimps endangered has been proposed. Meanwhile CITES, though a powerful law, isn't even being enforced in countries like Nigeria, where baby chimps are still captured, or in Egypt, where many of those same babies end up being sold as pets.

RIGHT *Stella and Gabe.*
OPPOSITE *Amy and Angie.*

"Things are in some ways worse today than when Carole was in Africa," says Geze Teleki. The atmosphere has become one of continuous compromise, driven by the financial interests of governments and corporations, and too often the wildlife is left to hang." Teleki feels that a lot of governments are more interested in making money off of animals than they are in protecting them: "Everything is measured by how much money you can make off it, and that's not really conservation."

While Carole Noon appreciated the potential of strong, well-crafted laws, many of them struck her as best suited to a more perfect world, one where both time and money were in better supply. She was both practical and often skeptical, which left

OF COURSE ONE CAN EASILY MAKE THE POINT THAT A GREAT MANY ANIMALS ARE FACING EXTINCTION IN THE COMING DECADES, FROM TIGERS AND RHINOCEROS, TO SEA TURTLES AND PARROTS..

OPPOSITE *Carole and Tammy.*
LEFT *Gabe.*

her inclined to look beyond legislation for solutions based on economics. She was impressed by the changes made to tuna harvesting, for example, when the public decided to boycott Starkist over the large number of dolphin deaths occurring during harvest operations. "What would happen if the World Bank said to Nigeria 'you won't be getting that 50 million dollars next quarter unless you clean up the killing of chimps.' How about a movement in the countries who buy and produce products from the timber from countries that are eating chimps or killing orangutans? What about 'bushmeat free' furniture?"

Of course one can easily make the point that a great many animals are facing extinction in the coming decades, from tigers and rhinoceros, to sea turtles and parrots. They, too, deserve better. But there's something especially dispiriting—and it will almost certainly be dispiriting for future generations—in the thought that in the end we couldn't muster the wherewithal to save even our closest kin.

beyond chimp city

BEYOND THE TRAGIC LOSS OF CHIMPS IN AFRICA, IN THE UNITED STATES WE CONTINUE TO ASK ONE OF THE MOST INTELLIGENT, MOST SOCIAL SPECIES ON EARTH TO SPEND THEIR LIVES IN CAGES, LARGELY ALONE AND AFRAID, SUBJECTED TO A WIDE RANGE OF DRUGS AND DISEASE. Clearly, things have been made better for chimpanzees through a series of legal stepping-stones, but there's much left undone.

The Chimpanzee Health Improvement, Maintenance, and Protection Act (CHIMP), passed in 2000, declared that all chimpanzees owned by the government would, upon retirement, be accepted into a federal sanctuary system. In 2002, the CHIMP Act established the Federal Sanctuary System, operated by Chimp Haven and overseen by the NIH.

In June 2013 the NIH announced that it would in coming years retire approximately 300 government-owned chimpanzees. Fifty chimpanzees will remain in research labs as a "reserve population." This is a significant step forward, and was cause for celebration. However, much work remains, including finding the funding to expand sanctuaries and retire the chimps, encouraging the government to retire the last 50 chimps, and addressing the fate of approximately 450 privately-owned laboratory chimps whose future is uncertain.

opening doors

Additionally, much hope was being held out for the more comprehensive Great Ape Protection and Cost Savings Act of 2011, which directed the phasing out of all chimpanzees in invasive research and, at the same time, prohibited future breeding of chimpanzees for such uses. Unfortunately, after working its way through Congress the bill died in committee in December of 2012.

On another legal front, Carole's pragmatism left her somewhat lukewarm about recent efforts in the United States to obtain actual legal rights for chimpanzees. She considered it both a great idea and at the same time a sizeable long shot. "In reality," she wrote, "chimpanzees are still being experimented on in labs, still being taken from their mothers to be trained for entertainment, still sit at roadside zoos to attract paying customers, and people can still keep them as pets. They are so far from any kind of rights that equal rights seems a bit esoteric to me." She preferred to aim lower: "Maybe spend some of those resources on getting a simple law passed that you can't keep a chimp as a pet or use them in entertainment. Still work with the government, but ask way less of them. Then get another law passed about biomedical research. Take some baby steps with measurable results, rather than trying for a giant leap, which isn't likely to occur without some huge gestalt."

MELODY

AT FIRST MEL WAS HAPPY JUST TO LOOK AROUND OR NAP. BUT LIKE ANY TODDLER, AS SHE GOT OLDER, SHE STARTED HAVING IDEAS OF HER OWN.

CAROLE NOON TRIED HER BEST TO PREVENT BABY CHIMPS FROM BEING BORN INTO SAVE THE CHIMPS FAMILIES, BELIEVING SANCTUARY RESOURCES WERE BEST USED TO SUPPORT EXISTING RESIDENTS AND TO RESCUE OTHERS IN NEED; NOT TO LAUNCH INTO FRESH, FIFTY-YEAR COMMITMENTS WITH NEW BABIES. But a series of failed vasectomies dashed all those best-laid intentions. ("This was quite the comeuppance for 'Ms. Against Captive Breeding,'" wrote Carole, referring to herself. "Hey, I love babies as much as the next guy, but do I want to bring baby chimps into this world and condemn them to a life of captivity measured in acres?") But babies they would have, and as everyone expected, they definitely livened up the sanctuary. For a chimp family (and in truth, for their human caregivers as well) the birth of a baby is an incredibly exciting event. Other adult females are especially eager to have a look, tiptoeing in as close as possible but carefully, trying to avoid being swatted and screamed at by a protective mother.

Melody—or Mel, as she's usually called—was born on July 12, 2007—daughter of a chimp named Megan, who at eight years old was barely past being a kid herself. Perhaps in part because of her own youth, though this certainly isn't clear, Megan showed no interest in the new baby, refusing even to touch her. This meant that the staff at Save the Chimps had to step in, providing round-the-clock care, including giving Mel a bottle every two hours. The trick in all this was figuring out how to raise little Mel without having her grow up too human.

With that in mind, staff decided to take her with them in a baby carrier on every errand at the chimp houses, be it to serve meals or clean the rooms, and in the process keeping her in close contact with other chimps. At first Mel was happy just to look around or nap. But like any toddler, as she got older—about the time she was eating food, needing a bottle only every eight hours—she started having ideas of her own. And that made the whole business a bit more

DANA

AS THOSE MALES WALKED AWAY FROM THE BUILDING, DANA ALL BUT YELLED, "WAIT UP GUYS—I'M COMING WITH YOU!"

OFFICIALLY, AT LEAST, AMONG ALL THE CHIMPANZEES CAROLE NOON DIDN'T HAVE ANY FAVORITES. But those who worked beside her over the years knew better; and among those chimps who held a special place in her heart, none had a bigger spot than Dana. One of the original Air Force chimps, among other things Dana became the chimp Carole looked to when it came to forming families. "I never made a move without her," Carole said, "often sending her in first during the introductions to gather more information."

The day the doors of the shelter building were opened to let the chimps access their island, Dana took a few steps outside and stopped, her eyes darting in every direction, looking utterly overwhelmed. "When she made eye contact with Waylon," Carole recalled, "she ran over to him and they hugged; I could barely see her surrounded by his great big arms." Shortly after that embrace, Gromek, Wes, Marty, Emory, and Garfield decided to explore, and as those males

walked away from the building, Dana all but yelled, "Wait up guys—I'm coming with you!" and rushed out to join them. Despite having serious arthritis, Dana and her companions explored the entire island, finally disappearing behind one of the small hills. "They couldn't see us, and we couldn't see them," said Carole. "I'm hoping this is one of those moments I will revisit if my life ever 'flashes before my eyes.'"

In 2003, after taking over the Coulston facility, Carole got a call from her staff in Florida saying Dana was having trouble walking. Carole caught a flight to Florida the next day, and by the time she landed at the sanctuary in Fort Pierce, Dana could no longer walk at all, able to move only by dragging the bottom half of her body around. Soon Dana was on her way to the University of Florida's Veterinary Hospital, calmly quaffing a cup of decaf coffee as the van rolled north up Highway 91. Beside the seat where Carole was sitting was a file folder with a one-page abbreviated version

of Dana's medical history, along with a more comprehensive file some two inches thick. In the pages of that bigger file were descriptions of all the experiments Dana had been subjected to over the years; incredibly, these included her having "donated" a kidney that was later transplanted into a baboon.

Carole was visibly upset, convinced that if she'd gotten her dear friend to the university sooner maybe she'd be up and around again by now. At one point she asked one of the doctors whether it would have made a difference had she gotten Dana there sooner. The doctor looked down at the two-inch file clutched in her hand. After a long, excruciating silence, he finally responded: "Yes," he said. "If you'd gotten her here about 40 years sooner. Then she wouldn't have had to live her whole life on cold, damp concrete."

By injecting dye into Dana's spinal cord, the doctors at the University of Florida were able to detect two lesions on her spine, but couldn't draw any conclusions. It was impossible to identify them as tumors or damaged discs, or something else

DANA GREETED HER KINDLY, LETTING HER GROOM HER AND THEN RETURNING THE FAVOR, AND ALSO LETTING CAROLE CHANGE THE WET BLANKETS SHE WAS SITTING ON.

entirely. Which also meant they couldn't predict Dana's future.

"Luckily," Carole later wrote, "I was in denial and didn't hear that Dana might be dealing with tumors or cancer. Dr. Bezner, the chimps' doctor [at Save the Chimps], told me about dogs whose back legs were useless due to damaged discs and after months and months of healing on their own walked again. But I didn't hear this either, because as we drove home from the university, I don't remember feeling the slightest bit of hope that Dana would ever walk again." When it came to this precious chimp, Carole had two things on her mind: one was bedsores, and the other, depression. If she wasn't moving around, how would they keep her wet blankets changed? Bedsores can lead to big problems, including deadly infections. How would the staff clean her cage? And if Dana couldn't move enough to protect herself, or run away from trouble, how could she stay on the island with

her group? The answer was, she couldn't. Yet taking her away from her family would almost certainly leave her depressed.

Dr. Bezner recalls the time when Dana first lost use of her legs: "She couldn't get up, and you know, as a vet the option of euthanasia is on your mind. But the first thing Dr. Noon said when we got the test results is 'how am I going to keep her intellectually entertained?' There was no discussion about putting her down—not because she was some crazy animal person, but because there was no reason to. Dana was perfectly happy; she was just concerned that Dana would get bored."

Late one day, after the staff and volunteers had left for the night, Carol asked visiting colleague Gloria Grow to go with her to the chimps' house to visit Dana. They found her sitting quietly on a pile of wet blankets, and that led Carole to take what is in this business a drastic measure. "She turned to me and said, 'I'm going to go in,'" recalls Gloria. "'I need you to open the door and lock me in.'" Gloria says that it was the first time she'd ever seen a human going in with a chimpanzee—at least an adult research chimp, one who'd been through so much. "But it was the most magical moment I've ever seen. She moved the blankets and made the bed more comfortable for Dana, and she did it as if she was going in with a dear old friend. Dana greeted her kindly, letting her groom her and then returning the favor, and also letting Carole change the wet blankets she was sitting on."

The only fly in the ointment was Pepsi, who was in the next cage over, and taking great exception to Carole being in the cage—yelling, pounding on the bars, in general putting everyone on edge, including Dana. At one point Dana tried to lift herself up to turn toward Pepsi, then looked at Carole and held out her hand for help. "Carole grabbed her hand," says Gloria, "then with Dana sitting up, the two of them started yelling at Pepsi together. From where I was, standing behind them, they looked like two sisters. Pepsi settled down. Dana hugged Carole. It was fabulous. It was one of the most beautiful things I've seen."

It wasn't just Carole who Dana would welcome, though. When a Save the Chimps caregiver named Chance moved to Florida from New Mexico, Dana all but swooned. ("She's such a shameless flirt," Carole explained.) He tickled and played with and generally pampered Dana. She got exclusive use of the tunnel connected to her cage so she could be outside every day. An elaborate system of special plastic pads was installed, lining the floor of her cage. And in the end only one bedsore showed up, which Dana allowed staff to treat with ointment.

It wasn't long before Dana had developed impressive upper body strength, which allowed her to

start using her arms as crutches. Once she was mobile enough, the staff started letting different chimps in with her, one at a time, to keep her company, to play with her, and to groom her. She really liked that.

Each day at the sanctuary the chimps are locked inside while they eat lunch, so that the staff can go out on the islands and scatter treats for them. "One day on a whim," said Carole, "or a psychic connection, or for no reason at all, I opened Dana's door to the island to see what she might do while the others were locked inside. I didn't realize until later that I opened her door a year to the day after Dana and I had taken our trip to the University." Dana struggled to get through the

door to the island with her useless legs, and then started scooting around. She hauled herself over to the windows of the chimps locked inside and greeted them. "Then she did something she hadn't done for a year. Dana stood. Yes, she stood up on her useless legs. It lasted a few seconds—not enough time for me to even call someone else over to verify what I saw."

So the staff started letting Dana out on the island each day while the others were inside eating lunch. At first she scooted about and then she'd take a step or two; with time she took more and more steps, going longer distances. After three months, Dana was walking through the door.

"It's no exaggeration," wrote Carole, "to say that my trusted partner in the formation of the Air Force group was Dana. Sometimes I felt guilty that I was exploiting her more than the lab ever did! She and I formed a special bond. I would do anything for her."

Carole's friend and colleague Theo Capaldo backs up that sentiment: "I think Dana and Carole were the cofounders of Save the Chimps. There was something about [Dana] that commanded your attention. She did it by the essence of her being."

Dana passed away in the spring of 2012, three years after one of her own most precious friends, Carole Noon.

Afterword

A Final Pant Hoot

WHEN ASKED TO REFLECT ON WHAT CAROLE NOON ACCOMPLISHED IN HER TOO-BRIEF LIFETIME, CELE-BRATED PRIMATOLOGIST GEZE TELEKI DOESN'T HESITATE TO USE THE WORD PHENOMENAL: "TO GET THAT SANCTUARY OFF THE GROUND WOULD'VE FOR MOST PEOPLE BEEN THE WORK OF SEVERAL LIFETIMES. This was a Mount Everest. But she never gave up, and she never gave in."

If it took an extraordinary amount of work to establish Save the Chimps in the first place, keeping it going—raising critical public funds, hiring staff, managing a small army of volunteers—would prove an equally big challenge. As those tasks grew Carole became increasingly tied to the grounds in Florida, sometimes not leaving for weeks at a time. Barbara Peterson remembers those days well: "Carole would call me and say something like 'I got my hair done today,' or 'I went shopping today and got some new clothes,' and I'd congratulate her."

The two women also spoke of the need to make sure the right leadership was in place to keep the sanctuary going if something happened to Carole. "This was ten years before she was diagnosed with cancer," recalls Peterson. "But even then, as much as she liked to run things, she began realizing she wasn't always going to be there. Chimps are like children; you have to make preparations for them in order to make sure they're going to be okay." When the current sanctuary director, Jen Feuerstein—a woman who'd been indispensable to the work at Coulston—first rose into an administrative role, it was in Barbara Peterson's words "an absolute godsend." Feuerstein's presence, along with that of veterinarian Jocelyn Bezner, communications director Triana Romero, and a host of other staff and tireless volunteers, is at the heart of what has allowed Save the Chimps to remain vibrant even after Carole's death in 2009. The basic work is as demanding as ever. Yet Carole would no doubt be pleased with the team of staff and volunteers that

RIGHT *Doc.*

OPPOSITE *Carole in Zambia.*

AS CAROLE SAID OVER AND OVER AGAIN THROUGHOUT THE YEARS, "CHIMPANZEES ARE AMAZING PEOPLE."

keeps rising to the challenge. One can't really escape the fact that, unexpected babies aside, when Carole Noon and Jon Stryker created Save the Chimps they were essentially building "old folks' homes." When Waylon died, it nearly brought Carole to her knees. Yet she reminded her staff that over the years she'd "learned how to use these emotions and channel them to do [her] very best for the chimps." She went on to say that while she'd love nothing more than to be "cemented" to the sanctuary "greeting Dana, Marty, Gromek and all the others each morning," she felt an urgency to hit the road and speak out on their behalf— both "the ones I know and the ones I don't know."

With that in mind, roughly a year before her own death, Carole started planning what she called the Speaking Out for Them Tour. "I need to tell people that Bobby used to sleep sitting up with his nose an inch from the wall of the cement cell where he lived alone. Nobody saw what I saw when the keys to the Coulston lab were placed in the palm of my hand. I am the witness." Even though such work would take her away from her beloved sanctuary, she didn't think the effort would be a lonely one, imagining somehow having the company of all the chimps that had passed since that fateful day

when she won custody of twenty-one former heroes from the American space program. "I'm thinking Tami and Tarzan, Faith, Emory, Karen, Doug, and Hanzie— who was the first chimp we lost to a broken heart—will be by my side. I expect my great big dear friend Waylon will be there too . . . standing at my side when I testify."

Carole often promised her staff that the chimpanzees they were caring for, who'd given their all to a system that gave them nothing in return but monkey chow and water, would, in the end, surprise them all. That happened all right, and with a depth and regularity that at times they could scarcely believe. As Carole said over and over again through the years: "Chimpanzees are amazing people." But while much attention has been paid to the flowering of these chimpanzees,

it is also worth noting the effect on their caregivers—a stunning testament to what acts of compassion can do for the hearts and lives of humans.

In 2005, Carole wrote a letter to Jon Stryker, musing about how difficult life can sometimes be. Referring to her favorite musician, Bob Dylan, she talked of the song "Forever Young," in which Dylan is listing things he hoped his kids would be able to have as they grew older—one of which was "to have a strong foundation when the winds of changes shift."

"I love Bob Dylan," she wrote, "and I love this song. But I can do without shifting winds. I hate change. I go through every one of them kicking and screaming with my knees locked, being dragged along, of course, by shifting winds. My experience has

been that every change (my divorce, the death of my parents, finding dear Hanzie dead in his cage from a heart attack) has given me something in return. I could not have diagnosed Phyllis and Marty and their heart conditions if I had never met Hanzie.

"Every change I have been dragged through, as scary as it was, turned out to be okay and often for the better. I knew taking over the Coulston Lab was going to cost me big time. It has. Who in their right mind would sign on to take over Coulston and then move the chimps to a new Chimp City in Florida they had to build? I guess me.

"Life is messy, no doubt about that. The amazing thing—and ask Dana if you don't believe me—is that all things are possible."

DR. CAROLE NOON PASSED AWAY EARLY ON MAY 2, 2009, OF PANCREATIC CANCER. She was in her home at Save the Chimps, within sight and sound of the chimpanzee islands, and in the company of her sisters. The sounds of the chimpanzees starting their day reverberated through the air as she slipped away. The chimps continued on as though it was any other day on the island.

Even without Carole's presence, Save the Chimps remains a bustling, dynamic sanctuary, offering safe haven for nearly three hundred chimpanzees, most of who came from lives of unimaginable fear and depression. As usual, today a fleet of golf carts is rolling around the grounds, carrying staff and volunteers and supplies to and from the shelter houses. Dr. Bezner is checking on a chimp with a bad skin rash. Jen Feuerstein is on the phone, listening as someone tells her about a pet chimp who needs sanctuary. Triana Romero is writing thank-you notes to donors, planning another outreach event, fielding calls from the media. The dogs are sound asleep in the office. And outside on the islands there are chimpanzees playing, grooming, lying on their backs under the bright Florida sky.

"One of the things I like about working here," Triana Romero says, "besides the chimps, are people's goodness, their compassion. We get a letter from a 90 year-old woman on social security who sends five dollars; or one of the donors, in his late 80s, diagnosed with bone cancer, calling to let us know we're a beneficiary. It's wonderful to find so many people who try to give back, who teach that to their children. I love that that's what I'm involved with every day."

Keeping this brilliant effort going in the years to come will take just such generosity. And in the long run it will take something more—a generosity of spirit in the culture at large. Nothing less will do if we are to see the day come when Save the Chimps is obsolete; if we truly want a future in which these sorts of refuges can be seen as bridges between an era when great apes were being terribly abused, to a time when we no longer put them in situations that lead to desperate and diminished lives. Over the years Carole Noon, Jane Goodall, and other passionate chimpanzee advocates have planted a great many seeds, feeding them with tenacity and passion; some, including Save the Chimps, ended up flowering in the most amazing ways. They have become a kind of garden, really—places where life is slightly kinder and brighter than it was before. Gardens worthy of our generous tending in the years to come.

OPPOSITE TOP LEFT *Alora sticks close to familiar steel and concrete while experiencing the feel—and taste—of grass for the first time.*

OPPOSITE TOP RIGHT *Carole.*

OPPOSITE BOTTOM LEFT *Yvette*

OPPOSITE BOTTOM RIGHT *Caregivers offering fruit to the chimpanzees.*

Save the Chimps

MISSION STATEMENT

To provide and build support for permanent sanctuary for the lifelong care of chimpanzees rescued from research laboratories, entertainment, and the pet trade.

CORE VALUES

1. Save the Chimps provides safety, privacy, lifetime care, freedom from exploitation, and the best captive care possible for the chimpanzees who live at the Sanctuary. The cornerstone of Save the Chimps' philosophy is that chimpanzees experience emotions such as joy, grief, anger, sorrow, pleasure, boredom, and depression.

2. Chimpanzees are persons, not commodities, and Save the Chimps will not buy, sell, trade, loan or conduct any commercial commerce of chimpanzees.

3. Each individual chimpanzee has equal value.

4. Save the Chimps does not endorse captive breeding and will, to the best of its ability, prevent reproduction among the resident chimpanzees through vasectomies and female birth control.

5. Save the Chimps limits access to the sanctuary to the board of directors, employees, consultants, volunteers and vendors, and allows visits or tours of other members of the public by invitation only.

6. Chimpanzees are accepted only in circumstances where Save the Chimps is assured they will not be replaced by the organization or individual giving over guardianship.

7. If it is in the best interest of an individual chimpanzee, Save the Chimps will consider placement of that chimp at another sanctuary able to provide equally high quality care for life.

8. Research is permitted only under limited circumstances. Such research must be observational and noninvasive and must demonstrate that is it of direct benefit to chimpanzees before approval by the leadership of Save the Chimps.

9. Save the Chimps respects all life and observes animal friendly practices that demonstrate our commitment to the environment, including efficient use of resources, reuse and/or recycling of products, preferential use of nontoxic substances.

You Can Help
Save the Chimps

Becoming a Save the Chimps member is one of the best ways to befriend the nearly 300 remarkable chimpanzees who call our sanctuary "home." Your membership gift helps to feed the chimps three fresh daily meals of fruits and vegetables; provide first-rate medical care for all the chimps; allow us to enrich their environment to provide a variety of activities, toys and treats that encourage natural behaviors; and help us maintain the 12 three-acre island homes that allow the chimps the space and freedom to wander to their hearts content.

In addition to giving the chimps the peaceful retirement they deserve, your membership gift entitles you to great benefits, including:

- Our annual "Speaking Out For Them" newsletter.
- Monthly e-news updates and photos of our beloved residents and life at the sanctuary.
- Opportunity to tour the Sanctuary on Member Day and witness first-hand nearly 300 chimpanzees roaming their islands and enjoying sanctuary life.

To become a member, make a donation, or join our "Adopt a Chimp" program, please visit our website at www.savethechimps.org.

Our work is only possible because of your generosity. Thank you!